# Gwen John
# An Interior Life

*Self-Portrait in a Red Blouse*. c.1900. Tate Gallery, London. Cat. 4.

# Gwen John
# An Interior Life

Cecily Langdale
and
David Fraser Jenkins

RIZZOLI
NEW YORK

*Acknowledgements*

I am indebted to many people for their assistance in the preparation of my forthcoming *catalogue raisonné* of the work of Gwen John. For their help with this exhibition specifically, I wish to express my gratitude to: Thomas F. Conroy; Roy Davis; Anthony d'Offay; Hilly Hoar; Michael Holroyd; John Hoole; A. D. Fraser Jenkins; Ben John; Sara John; Mary Elizabeth Laidlaw; Stefanie Maison; Krystyna Matyjaszkiewicz; Tony Mysak; Duncan Robinson; Melinda Kahn Tally; Robin Vousden; and the lenders, whose generosity has made this endeavour possible.

Cecily Langdale

I am grateful to the following people for their assistance, and for having been able to discuss the artist with them: Dr Thomas F. Conroy, Anthony d'Offay, the late Lady Clarke Hall, Michael Holroyd, the late Edwin John, Sara John, Stefanie Maison, and Mary Taubman.

David Fraser Jenkins

Extracts from Gwen John's letters to John Quinn, Ursula Tyrwhitt and Michel Salaman are reproduced by kind permission of the owners and copyright holders.

First published in the United States of America in 1986 by
RIZZOLI INTERNATIONAL PUBLICATIONS, INC.,
597 Fifth Avenue, New York, NY 10017



**Library of Congress Cataloging-in-Publication Data**

Langdale, Cecily.
Gwen John (1876–1939): an interior life.

Catalog of an exhibition held at the Barbican Art Gallery, London, 12 Sept.–3 Nov. 1985, the Manchester City Art Gallery, Dec. 1985–Jan. 1986, and the Yale Center for British Art, 26 Feb.–20 April 1986.
Bibliography: p.
Includes index.
1. John, Gwen, 1876–1939—Exhibitions. I. Jenkins, David Fraser. II. John, Gwen, 1876–1939. III. Barbican Art Gallery. IV. Manchester City Art Gallery. V. Yale Center for British Art. VI. Title.
ND497.J613A4 1986 759.2 85-18354
ISBN 0-8478-0681-2 (pbk.)



Printed in Great Britain by Balding + Mansell Limited

Published for the exhibition, *Gwen John: An Interior Life*, organized by Barbican Art Gallery in association with the Yale Center for British Art, New Haven.
Barbican Art Gallery, City of London: 12 September–3 November 1985.
Manchester City Art Gallery: 28 November 1985–26 January 1986.
Yale Center for British Art, New Haven: 26 February–20 April 1986.

# Contents

# Foreword

Recently Gwen John's work has become increasingly discussed but has been little seen. As a classic example of a woman artist in a male-dominated environment, she has been the subject of a book and a television film — unusual acclaim for *any* twentieth-century British artist — but the focus has always been on her life, with its tumultuous relationships and unlockable isolation, rather than on her art.

Her *oeuvre* was small. Some items were spread through purchase; others were seen during her lifetime only by a few friends and relations. An exhibition at the Matthiesen Gallery in 1946 briefly rekindled interest in her work, but with little visible since then it has been difficult to place her among her contemporaries or to judge the sustained quality of her art. The Barbican exhibition has gathered together about one third of her output in oils, to provide a rare display of her work and stand as a testimony to her artistic character.

Her teacher, Whistler, responded to her brother Augustus's remark about the strength of character in Gwen's work with: 'Character? What's that? It's tone that matters. Your sister has a fine sense of *tone*.' While Whistler judged her painting astutely from a technical point of view, he failed to appreciate that by concentrating so much upon the people and interiors that surrounded her, she engrossed herself spiritually in their characters. She thus sealed herself hermetically into 'an interior world', isolated from outside intrusions, revealing herself only as a reflection of her subjects. Her range of themes was narrow and the intensity of her concentration reveals the single-mindedness with which she directed her own life. '*Ma religion et mon art, c'est toute ma vie*', she wrote.

To all that have made this show possible, the lenders, friends and researchers, we extend grateful thanks. The two selectors separately floated the idea of a Gwen John retrospective and the merger of their talents has been most successful, with Cecily Langdale, author of the catalogue raisonné, contributing much valuable research, and David Jenkins bringing his experience of working on the John collection at the National Museum of Wales. The executors of Edwin John's estate have been most helpful, as has Anthony d'Offay. The lenders have kindly agreed to part with their pictures while the exhibition travels from Barbican Art Gallery to Manchester City Art Gallery and to the Yale Center for British Art. At New Haven, Gwen John's work will receive its first showing in a major East Coast gallery, and the occasion will mark a happy and fortunate collaboration in creating a transatlantic tour for a much overlooked painter.

John Hoole
Curator, Barbican Art Gallery

Duncan Robinson
Director, Yale Center for British Art

(opposite) *Girl Reading at the Window*. 1911. Museum of Modern Art, New York. Cat. 15.

*Self-Portrait*. Probably *c*.1907–9. Private collection. Cat. 65.

# A Summary Biography

**1876** Gwendolen Mary John was born on 22 June in Haverfordwest, Wales. She had two brothers—Thornton, born in 1875, and Augustus, born in 1878—and a sister Winifred, born in 1879. Their father Edwin was a solicitor in Haverfordwest.

**1884** Gwen's mother Augusta died, and the family moved to Tenby, where the children were educated.

**1895–8** Pupil at the Slade School of Fine Art, London, under Professor Fred Brown and Philip Wilson Steer. Augustus, although younger, had entered the school a year earlier and also stayed until 1898. He became the outstanding pupil of his generation, and a master of figure drawing. Contemporary pupils, all friends, included William Orpen, Ambrose McEvoy, Albert Rutherston (younger brother of William Rothenstein), and an outstanding group of girl students, Ida Nettleship, Grace Westray, Edna Waugh (Lady Clarke Hall), Gwen Salmond (Mrs Matthew Smith) and Ursula Tyrwhitt (Figs. 3–6). Few of Gwen's student works survive.

**1898** Awarded a prize for figure composition on leaving the Slade School.

September. Went to study at J. McNeill Whistler's new school, the Académie Carmen in Paris, with Ida Nettleship and Gwen Salmond, later joined by Michel Salaman: 'We have a very excellent flat . . . Gwen John is sitting before a mirror carefully posing herself—She has been at it for half an hour—It is for an "interior".' (Ida Nettleship to Michel Salaman, 1898.)

Visited Whistler's studio in Paris with Augustus. 'Character? What's that? It's *tone* that matters. Your sister has a fine sense of *tone*.' (Whistler's retort to Augustus John, recorded by the latter in *Chiaroscuro*, 1952, p. 66.)

**1899** February. Returned to London, and lived there until 1903, mostly in Bloomsbury and Bayswater.

**1900** Exhibited two paintings at the New English Art Club in London (Cat. 2, 4). This society arranged two exhibitions a year for its members and others, and was controlled by staff and students of the Slade School.

October. Visited Le Puy-en-Verlay, Burgundy, with Ambrose McEvoy (Fig. 5) and Augustus John. Gwen was then close to McEvoy, and learnt much from his interest in the technique of Old Master paintings.

**1901** Augustus married Ida Nettleship (Fig. 10).

**1901–2** Exhibited a single painting in both the April and November exhibitions of the New English Art Club in each of these years (Cat. 1, 3?).

**1903** March. Exhibited three paintings with Augustus's exhibition at the Carfax Gallery: 'Gwen has the honours, or *should* have . . . The little pictures to me are almost painfully charged with feeling.' (Augustus to William Rothenstein, in the latter's *Men and Memories*, 1932, vol. II, p. 65.)

Met Dorelia McNeill, who was studying at evening classes at Westminster School of Art. Despite Augustus's infatuation with Dorelia, she and Gwen went on a sketching expedition to south-west France in August, intending to go to Rome.

November. Arrived with Dorelia in Toulouse. Gwen completed three portraits of Dorelia, but not in time for the New English Art Club exhibition (Cat. 6, 7).

**1904** February. Moved with Dorelia to Paris, living at 19 boulevard Edgar Quinet, Montparnasse. They earned their living by modelling.

August. Augustus, with the help of Gwen, reclaimed Dorelia, who had moved to Bruges to live with another artist, whom she had met in Paris.

Gwen John met Auguste Rodin (Fig. 19) in the studio of a sculptor. She began to model for him, and became his mistress. Rodin posed her as a *Muse* (also called *Venus Climbing the Mountain of Fame*, see Fig. 18) for a monument to Whistler, who had died in 1903, commissioned by the International Society of Sculptors, Painters and Gravers, of which Whistler had been President. The monument was never cast in bronze.

**1905** Continued to earn her living by modelling for women artists as well as for Rodin.

*The Student*. 1903–4. Manchester City Art Galleries. Cat. 6.

(right) *Chloe Boughton-Leigh*. 1910. Leeds City Art Galleries. Cat. 14.

**1906** Moved to 7 rue St. Placide, Montparnasse. Met the poet Rainer Maria Rilke, who was Rodin's secretary until 1907, and met him again in 1908, becoming a friend.

**1907** March. Moved to 87 rue du Cherche-Midi, Montparnasse. On 14 March Ida John died in hospital in Paris, after birth of her son Henry.

Met Chloe Boughton-Leigh in Paris, and she and Gwen painted each other.

**1908** April. Exhibited a self-portrait (Cat. 9) and the portrait of Chloe Boughton-Leigh (Cat. 8) at the New English Art Club: 'Gwen's pictures are simply staggering, I have put the prices up to £50. They will surely sell.' (Augustus John to Dorelia, 10 April 1908.)

'I am drawing myself nude in the glass, or rather painting—watercolour mixed with Chinese white.' (Gwen John to Ursula Tyrwhitt, 30 July 1908.)

**1909** Moved to 6 rue de l'Ouest, Montparnasse.

Painted Fenella Lovell, nude and clothed (Cat. 12, 13), paying her to model (continuing to 1910).

Winter. Exhibited *The Student* (Cat. 6) at the New English Art Club.

**1910** Made two etchings, her only prints (Cat. 72). Painted a second portrait of Chloe Boughton-Leigh (Cat. 14).

Augustus recommended Gwen to the New York collector, John Quinn (Fig. 16), who was already buying the work of Augustus. Quinn offered to buy a painting by Gwen: 'I am afraid you must wonder why the picture you ordered has not arrived . . . I am doing one which will be more agreeable.' (Gwen John to John Quinn, 28 July 1910.)

Summer. Exhibited two paintings at the New English Art Club.

**1911** Moved to top floor flat at 29 rue Terre Neuve, Meudon (Fig. 21), twelve minutes by train from Paris, and near Rodin's country house. Retained apartment at rue de l'Ouest as a studio.

November. Exhibited *Girl Reading at the Window* (Cat. 15) at the New English Art Club.

'I paint a good deal, but I don't often get a picture done—that requires, for me, a very long time of a quiet mind, and never to think of exhibitions.' (Gwen John to Mrs Sampson, 5 December 1911; quoted in Michael Holroyd, *Augustus John*, 1974, vol. I, p. 113.)

**1912** 'As to whether I have anything worth expressing that is apart from the question. I may never have anything to express, except this desire for a more interior life.' (Gwen John to Ursula Tyrwhitt, 4 September 1912(?).)

October. Began Roman Catholic instruction at Meudon.

November. From this time John Quinn sent her a regular annual allowance, in return for paintings.

**1913** February. Armory Show at New York included her *Girl Reading at the Window* (Cat. 15) lent by John Quinn, who was one of the organizers of this first exhibition of modern art in America.

Received into Roman Catholic Church. Promised to paint a series of copy portraits of Mère Marie Poussepin, the founder of the Order, for the Convent of the Sisters of Charity at Meudon.

**1914** December. Augustus John called at Meudon to persuade Gwen to return to Britain during the war, but she would not leave: 'I have decided to stay. Every day after seeing the Gare Montparnasse crammed . . . I felt more and more disinclined to go.' (Gwen John to Ursula Tyrwhitt, 10 December 1914.)

**1915** Summer. Visited Pléneuf, near St. Malo in Brittany, and made out-of-doors portrait drawings of the local children. She travelled there with Ruth Manson, an English friend from Paris, and her daughter. (She visited Pléneuf every summer for the next six years.)

**1916** Made copies of photographs of Allied war leaders to send to John Quinn, and to sell.

March. Two paintings (including *La Petite Modèle*, Cat. 23), nine gouaches and a portfolio of drawings delivered to John Quinn in New York.

'. . . a picture ought to be done in one sitting or at most two. For that one must paint a lot of canvases probably and waste them.' (Gwen John to Ursula Tyrwhitt, 3 August 1916; quoted by Mary Taubman, *Gwen John*, 1968, p. 17.)

**1917** On 17 November Rodin died. Gwen John had not been personally close to him for some years, but had continued to write to him incessantly, and was profoundly disturbed by his death.

**1918** During the summer at Pléneuf discovered an abandoned house, the Manoir de Vauxclair, and lived there, trying to persuade John Quinn to buy it.

'I should like to exhibit a lot together. My last drawings look much better if they are seen a lot together. It is difficult to know why. Perhaps in looking at 1 or 2 the details would be noticed too much or something like that.' (Gwen John to Ursula Tyrwhitt, 6 September 1918.)

**1919** Lived at the Manoir de Vauxclair, Pléneuf, for most of the year: 'It is difficult to describe the Château of Vauxclair. It is not grand at all. It has a beauty of its own, rather sad. It is four or five centuries old. It has wonderful trees and the gardens are beautiful

Fig. 1. Augustus John. *Gwen John Seated by a Fireplace*. *c*.1897. Private collection.

*Interior (Rue Terre Neuve)*. Probably early to mid 1920s. Manchester City Art Galleries. Cat. 44.

*Girl Praying*. Probably c.1930. Mr and Mrs D. Little. Cat. 51.

too; of course, all grown savage now, but that gives them more charm to me.' (Gwen John to John Quinn, 6 October 1919.)

**1920** September. Jeanne Robert Foster (Fig. 15), a poet and friend of John Quinn, visited Paris and spent some time with Gwen John, going to art galleries with her.

**1921** Visited Pléneuf for the last time.

July. Travelled to Britain to stay with the poet, Arthur Symons (Cat. 103) and his wife Rhoda at Wittersham, Kent: 'Yes, my drawings are much better seen in sets. When I saw them hung on the walls at the Symons' separately I was disappointed.' (Gwen John to Ursula Tyrwhitt, 20 July 1921.)

August. Met John Quinn in Meudon. Quinn called on the Mother Superior at the convent and arranged to buy the best version of *Mère Poussepin* (Cat. 17).

September. Painted a portrait of Jeanne Robert Foster, who stayed on in Paris after John Quinn had returned to New York.

December. *Mère Poussepin* and *Girl in Blue* (Cat. 17) delivered to John Quinn, together with paintings for Jeanne Robert Foster.

**1922** 'I am quite in my work now and think of nothing else. I paint till its dark . . . Every day is the same.' (Gwen John to John Quinn, 27 March 1922.)

*Modern English Artists* exhibition at the Sculptors' Gallery, New York, included five paintings and ten drawings by Gwen John lent by John Quinn, in a group show with Augustus John, Jacob Epstein, Wyndham Lewis, James Dickson Innes and Henri Gaudier-Brzeska.

September. Exhibited at the Salon d'Automne, Paris.

**1923** Exhibited at the Salon des Tuileries and Salon d'Automne, Paris.

September–October. Met John Quinn and his assistant Henri-Pierre Roché in Paris (Fig. 20).

**1924** John Quinn died on 21 July: 'I can't paint because if I painted it would be to finish some things which were going to "John" and it gives me pain.' (Gwen John to Jeanne Robert Foster, 28 September 1924.)

September. Exhibited at the Salon des Tuileries, Paris.

**1925** 'I am in love with the atmosphere of Meudon church and the people who go to church there have a charm for me (especially when I don't speak to them . . .).' (Gwen John to Jeanne Robert Foster, 22 February 1925.)

*New English Art Club Retrospective Exhibition* in London included four paintings by Gwen John, lent from collections in Britain.

**1926** May–July. Retrospective exhibition of Gwen John's work held at the New Chenil Galleries, London. Forty-four paintings and watercolours, and four albums of drawings listed in the catalogue.

'Your letter makes me happy and gives me encouragement to go on having my solitude (which sometimes seems a sort of obstinacy).' (Gwen John to Michel Salaman, 3 June 1926.)

Autumn. Purchased bungalow and garden at 8 rue Babie, Meudon (Fig. 22). Flat at rue Terre Neuve retained as a studio, but eventually lived mainly at rue Babie.

December. Visited for the first time Jacques Maritain and his wife Raïssa, who lived at Meudon. Gwen John became attached to Raïssa's sister Véra Oumançoff and later sent her drawings once a week as a present, continuing through 1928 and 1929.

**1927** Augustus John bought Yew Tree Cottage at Burgate Cross in Wiltshire for Gwen, near his home at Fryern Court. She visited it in June, but returned to Meudon in September: 'My cottage is lovely . . . I count on you not to tell anyone. I will not be troubled by people.' (Gwen John to Ursula Tyrwhitt; quoted by Richard Buckle in the exhibition catalogue, *Ursula Tyrwhitt*, Ashmolean Museum, Oxford, 1974.)

**1929** Visited by Maynard Walker, a dealer from New York who proposed an exhibition; and by John Quinn's sister Julia Anderson, with her daughter.

**1930s** During the 1930s painted numerous tiny copies of a photograph of Saint Teresa of Lisieux with her sister (Cat. 121).

Augustus's son Edwin stayed frequently in Paris and visited Gwen.

'Just imagine a little bit of ground enclosed by walls and absolutely covered with trees and woods, except the path that goes from the gate to the little wooden shed which she uses as a studio and which, at the same time, is where she lives.' (Guillaume Lerolle, representative of the Carnegie Institute, Pittsburgh; typescript of his report to the Carnegie Institute. Tate Gallery archive.)

**1939** Gwen John died in Dieppe, which she had visited for an unknown reason.

A full biography is given in Susan Chitty's *Gwen John*, 1981. This summary is indebted to that book, and to Michael Holroyd's *Augustus John*, vol. I 1974, vol. II 1975. Gwen John's letters to John Quinn belong to the New York Public Library; her letters to Ursula Tyrwhitt and Michel Salaman belong to the National Library of Wales, Aberystwyth.

# Gwen John: An Appreciation

DAVID FRASER JENKINS

Both in her life and in her reputation Gwen John is unique in modern art, and her painting, despite some general similarities to the work of other artists in London and Paris, came to bear upon a particular area of human feeling. Several other Post-Impressionist artists were grossly undervalued in their day—most notoriously Cézanne, who was known in Britain only after his death—but it is odd that Gwen John herself consciously resisted recognition. Her self-neglect was always remarked, and this refers as much to her routine of working as to her domestic life. There was only one exhibition of Gwen John's work in her lifetime, at the New Chenil Galleries in London, in 1926. At her death in 1939 she still possessed the great bulk of her paintings. Were it not for her nephew Edwin, who inherited this collection, and as an artist knew how to attend to it, it is conceivable that most of her output might have been lost. Her finest paintings were made in the ten years between 1915 and 1925, in Paris and in Meudon, a suburb of Paris, at a time when her contemporary artist friends in London were enjoying successful careers. She cultivated privacy, and a sense of privacy is one of the dominant feelings of her painting.

This privacy has become an irony for today's viewer, since her most secret life has been presented to sight in the biography by Susan Chitty published in 1981, which has paraphrased her letters to the much older and very celebrated sculptor Auguste Rodin, with whom she had a love affair. Gwen John's total and violent commitment to Rodin endured for about the last thirteen years of his life (he died in 1917), and her flood of correspondence to him is preserved in the archive of his museum in Paris. Nevertheless, the overwhelming importance for her of this love had at the time been a secret from all but the *demi-monde* circle of Rodin's models and entourage, and, as far as her former friends in London could acknowledge, from the time that she settled in Paris, aged twenty-seven, in 1904, she might as well have been alone. She was not entirely reclusive, and visited the Salons and other art exhibitions in Paris, but she always worked in solitude, and took only the little that she wanted from the great years of the modern movement in the arts.

There was a major change in her technique during the years 1910 to 1915 (her production then was slow), and a gradual alteration through her later period. She seems to have painted little after her exhibition in 1926. In subject she was extraordinarily consistent. Around 1915, at the close of her relationship with Rodin, she began to complete a greater number of paintings, encouraged by her one patron, the New York collector John Quinn (whom she finally met at Meudon in 1921 and 1923, but otherwise knew only by letter). Her subjects in these later

*The Japanese Doll*. Probably early to late 1920s. Ben John. Cat. 45.

*The Teapot (Interior: Second Version)*. c.1915–16. Yale University Art Gallery. Cat. 19.

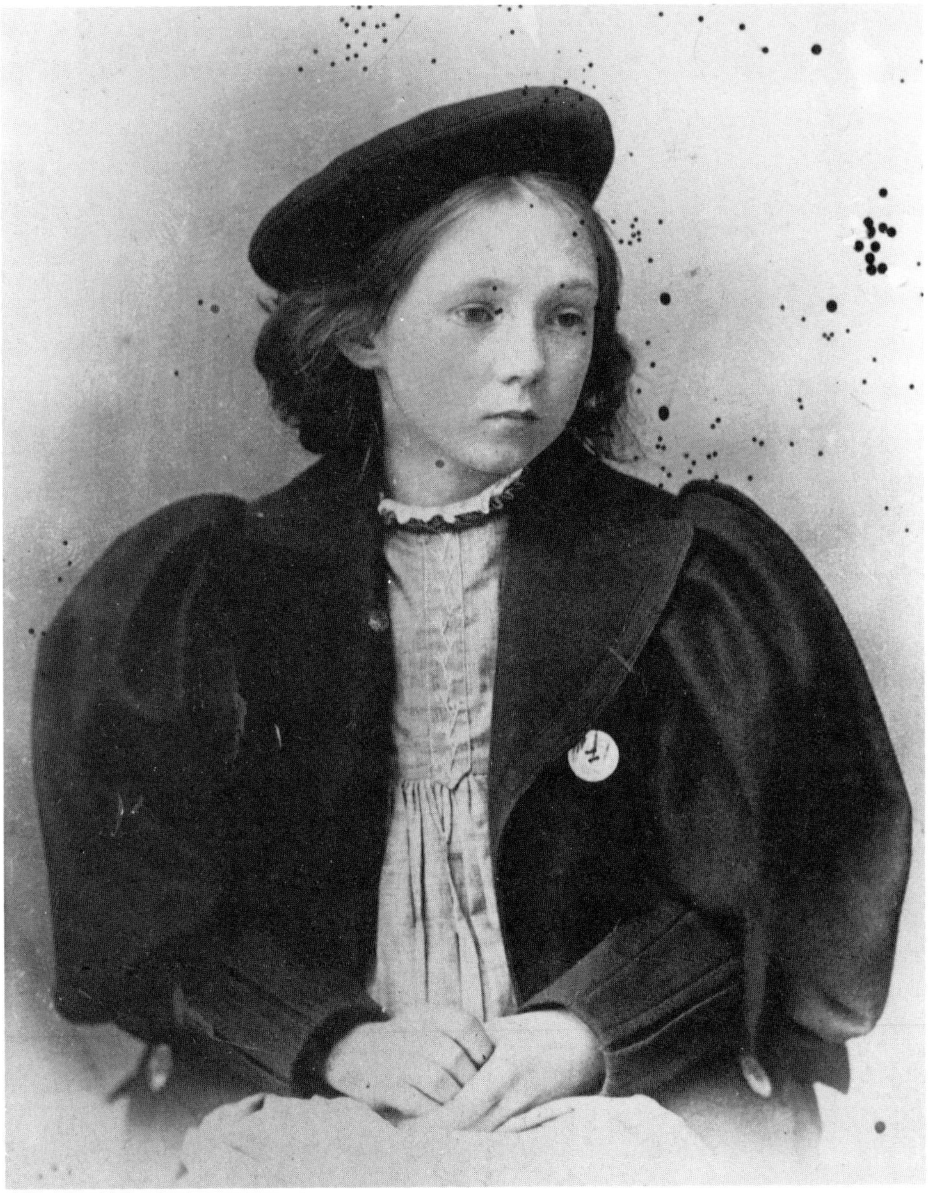

Fig. 2. Gwen John as a child.
Michael Holroyd.

paintings, as before, are three-quarter length young women and girls, seated in a bare interior. These are not exactly portraits, as all the supporting properties of personality have been taken away, and it is clear that the subjects were not commissioning the work. Many are of the same unknown model. Formal qualities of design, control of tone and unity of surface and depth are the principal components of the paintings, to the disregard of realism and of what is commonly meant by drawing. But it is as figures that these paintings are appreciated, figures who appear to be presented completely honestly, since without guile or advantage, and yet who as people are unknowable, as their personalities cannot be grasped. The figure holds the eye of the spectator by means of the slow deliberation of the touches of paint, but at the same time that it is pondered the metaphor between touch and human character is dispersed and lost.

So much about Gwen John confounds the historian of modern art that it is almost to be expected that the one pupil of the Slade School in the 1890s (the most promising new generation of talent, but rather provincial) who came closest to art in Paris and could have mediated between the two worlds, as had Whistler, was this one, who worked alone and for herself. Her period at the Slade School ended in the summer of 1898, and that autumn she went, along with two other girls from

Fig. 3. Augustus John. *Grace Westray*. c.1900. Cambridge, Fitzwilliam Museum.

Fig. 4. Augustus John. *Ursula Tyrwhitt*. c.1900. Cambridge, Fitzwilliam Museum.

the Slade, to study in Paris for almost six months. Their London professors did not approve.

For Gwen John this was an extension of her life in London, and even further away from parental and professorial supervision. Students could enrol without difficulty at Colarossi's or Julian's, but the point of this expedition was to attend Whistler's newly opened and suddenly popular Académie Carmen. Unlike the Slade, it was a school of painting rather than drawing. Whistler, who was regarded as an Impressionist, was the opposing pole of modern art in London to Burne-Jones, who in drawing was like the Italian Old Masters, and these three girls had opted for the rival to the Slade. Beyond the development of her painting, for Gwen John it was also an example of a new life. In Paris foreigners and artists were acceptable, and many records of a refuge there before 1914, such as Middleton Murry's autobiography, celebrate this chance to live alone.

The following four and a half years, until 1903, were the last that she was to live in Britain. Although it was then that she first exhibited, little detail is known of her life in flats in Bloomsbury and Bayswater. It was a time that she herself remembered as unpleasant, and sufficient justification for residing abroad.

She had wanted to leave her native Pembrokeshire, and she wanted to leave London, where she had chosen mostly to live alone. She eventually wanted to leave Paris, and moved to the suburb of Meudon, then a village. Going beyond the need for privacy in which to work was her desire to live as an exile, without a sense of place or family, in an international city such as Paris. In the limited terms of technique she was an Anglo-French artist, but in her front to the world presented by the completed paintings she did not share responsibility with anyone. The withdrawal from outside reference was progressive, along with an enriching of the area of mind that remained at core.

In 1900, after her return from her first brief visit to Paris, her painting resembled that of other members of the New English Art Club. Its similarity to

*Flowers*. Probably late 1910s. Manchester City Art Galleries. Cat. 22.

*Girl in Profile*. Probably late 1910s. National Museum of Wales, Cardiff. Cat. 25.

Fig. 5. Edna Clarke Hall. *Ambrose McEvoy*. *c*.1900. Etching. Cardiff, National Museum of Wales.

Fig. 6. Edna Clarke Hall. *Gwen John*. *c*.1900. Drawing. Cardiff, National Museum of Wales.

Whistler's should not be exaggerated, and lies chiefly in the subdued colour. At that time she gave a lesson in oil painting to her friend Edna Clarke Hall, who otherwise painted in watercolours (Fig. 8). She spent almost all the time instructing her how to prepare colours on her palette with scrupulous cleanliness: this was Whistler's method, to prepare exactly a harmony of pigment before transferring it to the canvas. Her attitude to her subjects was otherwise much as that of William Rothenstein (Fig. 7), and both displayed a general kind of English realism within a late Victorian tradition. It was the heyday of the domestic interior. These paintings made a virtue of lack of ambition in subject, but Gwen John's stopped short of the story-telling of Rothenstein's interiors, and were not as imaginative as Whistler's. (In the latter's studio in Paris she had probably seen his tiny oil studies such as *Harmony in Blue and Gold: the Little Blue Girl* (1894–1903, Fig. 9), but it was not until much later that she took up this aesthetic.) Many of Gwen John's paintings from this early period are lost, but there is some variety of style in those that are known. Her first two paintings seen in public, at the New English Art Club in 1900, *Portrait of Mrs Atkinson* (Cat. 2) and *Self-Portrait in a Red Blouse* (Cat. 4), reveal her prolonged observation and control of tone, and are better than the slightly more contrived paintings that followed in the next few years.

This period was ended by the walking expedition across France with Dorelia McNeill in the autumn of 1903. It is odd that Gwen John chose Rome as a destination. The trip has the appearance of an elopement, taking Dorelia, whom she, the first of the family, had met only that year, away from her brother Augustus (who was to become Dorelia's lover). Rome was no draw for the non-academic artist, and perhaps was no more than the illusory destination of the

traveller. They got no further than Toulouse, but the three months they spent together there were crucial. Gwen John began five paintings, including three completed portraits of Dorelia painted by artificial light, in a return to her style of 1900. They were living on their own, away from all acquaintances and away from London. She was working successfully and gave up the idea of having things ready by the deadline of an exhibition, which she had always before found painful and incompatible with her aim for perfection. This was to be the model for the remainder of her life.

By going to provincial France, Gwen had separated herself from her brother. Augustus was not yet well known to the public, but was the dominating personality of their circle of Slade School artists. Promiscuous in allegiances to Old Masters from Rembrandt to Goya, he was just then concentrating on drawing, and was held back for some years until he had freed himself from a clumsy technique of oil painting. In London Gwen and Augustus had drawn side by side, but there are no pairs of such works surviving. Augustus's *Ardor* (1904, Fig. 11), a small head of Dorelia, was painted after she had returned from the Toulouse episode. In comparison to Gwen's *Dorelia in a Black Dress* (Cat. 7), it is a draughtsman's portrait, whose flicker of sensual expression is achieved, like the dimples and curly hair, by a twist of the hand. The likeness has been seized, attractively, with echoes of Rubens and Daumier. Gwen's portrayal of Dorelia was not so much seized as approached, while the latter stood with an expression of face and body that was a response to prolonged attention from the artist. The pose and spacing are unconventional, and bring to mind no other artist. There is no need for a theatrical title, as the confrontation is direct and deep. Both paintings are evidence of genuine emotion, and the comparison is not quite fair to Augustus whose most ambitious works were figure groups, and who for the sake of his range should not be judged by one painting at a time. In terms of application, the drawing of *Dorelia in a Black Dress* is less stylish and more subservient to colour than that by Augustus. The shapes are summarized more clearly, and the hands look strong and fleshy. Occasionally Gwen would try Augustus's manner, as in the confident pose of the self-portrait in the National Portrait Gallery (Cat. 5), or the unusually dramatic drawing *Étude pour 'Les Suppliantes'* (Cat. 73). The rhythmic elegance of

Fig. 7. William Rothenstein. *The Browning Readers*. 1900. Bradford City Art Gallery.

Fig. 8. Edna Clarke Hall. *Still Life with a Print after Titian*. c.1900. Private collection.

Fig. 9. James McNeill Whistler. *Harmony in Blue and Gold: the Little Blue Girl*. c.1894–1903. Washington, Freer Art Gallery.

*Girl Holding a Book*. Probably late 1910s to early 1920s. Smith College Museum of Art, Northampton, Mass. Cat. 31.

*Girl with Cat*. Probably late 1910s to early 1920s. Metropolitan Museum of Art, New York. Cat. 28.

Fig. 10. Augustus, Ida (holding David) and Gwen. 1901. Michael Holroyd.

Augustus's line could not readily be translated into paint, and was a product of his imagination, often uniting entire assemblies of his family posing in a landscape. It is only rarely that Gwen's paintings show something that was not directly in front of her. Many critics have assessed Gwen and Augustus John as opposites. He himself wrote that they were 'much the same, really'. In character it is true that both were egotistical and passionate, but in their art his symbolism is directly contrary to the realism of her earlier paintings.

The Johns were part of the same generation as those artists who in London became the Camden Town Group. It is appropriate to compare Gwen John to one of these, Harold Gilman, who was born in the same year, not because they knew each other's work especially well, but because their roots in the Slade School and the tradition of Whistler and Degas were similar. Gilman's paintings such as *The Nurse* (*c.*1908, Fig. 12) demonstrate that Gwen John's paintings, like the earlier version of *Chloe Boughton-Leigh* (1907, Cat. 8), come near to what was a group advance in Britain. Before this their work had not been similar, since Gilman's was more narrative, and influenced by his time in Spain. It is the character of the portrait that is relevant, and its presentation through a restricted range of tones and a calculated design. By 1910 Gilman was painting with the dry touches of strong and speckled colour typical of the Camden Town artists, and he practised the modern subjects of the Group, but there is still an appropriate comparison in his portraits. Gwen John's *La Petite Modèle* (1915, Cat. 23) is made up of touches of chalky, opaque paint, in which there are no drawn lines, and the surface structure is much the same throughout. This might describe Gilman's *The Blue Blouse, Portrait of Elène Zompolides* (1910, Fig. 13), but he uses light and shade, and contrast of colour to give expression to the sitter. None of Gwen John's later oils gives the name of the sitter, apart from Mère Poussepin (Cat. 17, 20) and the exceptional portrait of Bridget Bishop (Cat. 50). The oddity of her design is evident

Fig. 11. Augustus John. *Ardor* (Dorelia McNeill). 1904. Manchester City Art Galleries.

Fig. 12. Harold Gilman. *The Nurse.* c.1908. Birmingham Museum and Art Gallery.

Fig. 13. Harold Gilman. *The Blue Blouse, Portrait of Elène Zompolides.* 1910. Leeds City Art Galleries.

in comparison to Gilman's: it is typical that her subjects are off-centre or leaning, and half-way between sitting and standing. Details of dress and background are obscure, and the scrawny hands that seem too large are a rival expression to the face. The most distorted presentation is the small study of the model Fenella Lovell clothed (1909, Cat. 13), which is to some extent relaxed in the nude version of the same subject (1909, Cat. 12), where the sitter's shoulders and arms are more balanced.

Gwen John was not aware of these paintings of Gilman's, which were not exhibited in Paris. The similarities are a coincidence resulting from a common origin, but the comparison points out her special qualities. Her paint is drier and more chalky than that of the Camden Town artists, and she made up the colours herself. The method of application necessarily changed, since the paint was mostly dabbed in touches rather than brushed along (although some paintings, such as the *Girl in Profile* (Cat. 25), have areas of furious attack). There is no drawing with the paint and no sense of atmosphere through glazing, no reflections or dappled shade. The liveliness that follows from a sense of movement is replaced by stasis, and, in the composition of paint, the figure and the background are the same. The cloaks and still lifes, and the zig-zag outline of the clenched fingers, are so merged with background as sometimes to appear to be abnormal shapes. The greatest difference from Gilman is in the palette, since Gwen John did not use contrasts of colour but tonal resemblances.

The appreciation of Gwen John has been battered not only by knowledge of her private life, but by the changes in art criticism resulting from the feminist movement. There has been no directly feminist criticism of her work, although she has been recognized in the anthologies and included (her paintings from John Quinn's collection) in the important American exhibitions of women artists. Some unspecific criticism has, however, been startlingly relevant, in the contrast

*Study of Marigolds*. Probably late 1910s to early 1920s. Private collection. Cat. 107.

*A Corner of the Artist's Room in Paris*. 1907–9. Sheffield City Art Galleries. Cat. 10.

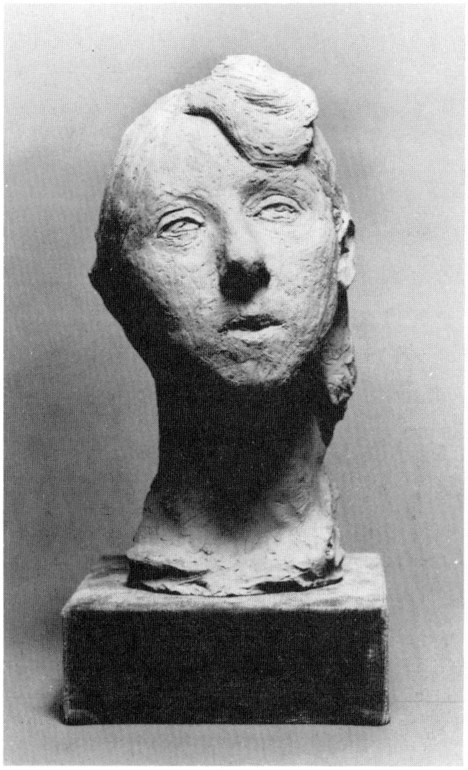

Fig. 14. Ursula Tyrwhitt. *Gwen John*. 1907. Terracotta bust. Oxford, Ashmolean Museum.

between Gwen and her brother, and the aims of her later painting and its imagery.

It is only a parody of feminist art history to believe that a woman artist failed to receive notice because of suppression by her male rivals, but it is worth emphasizing the efforts of those in her circle in Britain to make her known, and to find an audience for her painting. That she was not absolutely forgotten in her lifetime was due to Augustus. He was financially well off after about 1913, but could hardly have supported her; help would not have been accepted and money was not so much a problem while she was able to model, however unpleasant that was at times. It was Augustus who persuaded John Quinn in 1910 to buy a painting, not seen, on the evidence of his enthusiasm (and possibly of examples of her work belonging to Augustus). When by 1920 Quinn had grown tired of Augustus he nevertheless continued to pay Gwen an allowance, usually for work not yet completed, and he gave her vital encouragement until his death in 1924.

Quinn, who was an experienced collector of modern art, asked only for examples of Gwen John's own style. He had no wish to make her into anything other than herself, and sought her opinion of various exhibitions which he could not travel from New York to see. He asked for a portrait of his friend Jeanne Foster, but seems not to have been especially put out when the sittings were unsuccessful. Eventually, he owned about eighteen paintings and some fifty drawings by Gwen John, and this was the only group of works that his heirs partly retained in the family when his collection was sold.

Gwen John had no other support as strong as Quinn's, but some of the few paintings she exhibited in London, and then later in Paris, were bought by collectors. At the New Chenil Galleries in 1926 there were a number of purchases, and the year before the organizers of the New English Art Club retrospective exhibition had been able to borrow four paintings from English collections. Some sitters such as Chloe Boughton-Leigh were probably given their own portraits. An anonymous donor gave two paintings to the Contemporary Art Society in 1911.

Fig. 15. Jeanne Robert Foster. *c.*1923. Private collection.

Fig. 16. John Quinn. *c.*1923. Private collection.

These were accepted by the Tate Gallery in 1917, at the same time as the first of Augustus's paintings. Charles Rutherston bought her work at the Salon d'Automne of 1924, and Professor Fred Brown (of the Slade School), Frances Cornford and Louise Salaman owned works by 1925. The collectors were all acquaintances, but they acquired a good proportion of what she had exhibited before the New Chenil Galleries show.

Published criticism of her work was favourable, particularly of one of her rare early exhibits, at the New English Art Club in 1908: 'The portrait of Miss C. Boughton-Leigh seems to us one of the greatest achievements in the exhibition because of this sincerity' (T. Martin Wood, *Studio*, 44, 1908). Laurence Binyon wrote similarly of her exhibit *The Student* (Cat. 6) in the 1909 exhibition. The retrospective exhibition of the New Chenil Galleries was reviewed by Mary Chamot (*Country Life*, 19 June 1926) under the title 'An Undiscovered Artist'. While admitting that Gwen John was already known in Britain to a few people, Mary Chamot was the first to write of her later work, and in effect introduced the whole range of subsequent criticism. She pointed out the careful structure and the extreme beauty of the colouring in these paintings, and warned that it should not be concluded that the human content was of no consequence. The first biographical account was that of Sir John Rothenstein (1952), who outspokenly judged her 'one of the finest painters of our time and country', and who thus became the last writer to claim justly that she was little known.

Rothenstein had spoken about Gwen to his father, William Rothenstein, and to Augustus and Dorelia John, and was given access by Edwin John to all her papers, although he could not see her letters in the Musée Rodin. He used this information, in the manner of the other biographies in his 'Lives', to present her as an individual. Knowing of her life, and of the change in her later work, he commented on its exceptional strength that, 'the wisdom she gained from her emotional and spiritual ordeals was little by little embodied in her deeply rooted art.' Is this so? Is

*Girl Holding a Rose*. Probably late 1910s to early 1920s. Paul Mellon Collection, Upperville, Virginia. Cat. 35.

*The Convalescent*. Probably late 1910s to mid 1920s. Private collection. Cat. 42.

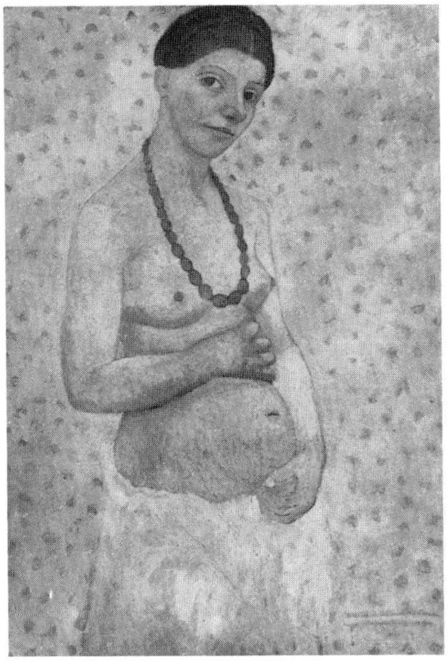

Fig. 17. Paula Modersohn-Becker. *Self-Portrait on Sixth Wedding Anniversary*. 1906. Bremen, Ludwig L. Roselius Sammlung.

it justifiable to suppose a transfer from her own mental life in these portraits, and if so how is it that such human feeling is contained within them? Recent critics have also felt something like this, for example Suzi Gablik in an appreciative review of Anthony d'Offay's 1976 exhibition: 'what comes across from these paintings is a dedicated concentration, a private incandescence of spirit that is enthralling.' It is a matter of observation that Gwen John's painting has been more greatly admired by women than by men: this is true of those who have written about her, students who have studied her work and even of casual visitors to exhibitions. Perhaps her personality can be sympathetically shared, and criticism can now more easily value feminine elements without condescension.

Unlike her older contemporary, Käthe Kollwitz, Gwen John had no interest in political issues, and her withdrawal from society was neither radical nor conservative. She did, however, by birth belong to that first great generation of women artists, those born in the 1870s and 1880s. It is possible that Gwen John met Paula Modersohn-Becker, her exact contemporary, in the studio of Rodin in 1905—but there is no evidence, although Rainer Maria Rilke, Modersohn-Becker's brother-in-law, was a friend in common. The two women shared an overwhelming need to escape from family by living in Paris to work, and Modersohn-Becker had temporarily left her husband in Germany. Unlike Gwen John, she was inspired by Gauguin to a residual symbolism, but her painting is also almost exclusively of the female figure, often nude, shown with images of birth. She painted herself, nude and pregnant, titled *Sixth Wedding Anniversary* in 1906 (Fig. 17), at a time when, extraordinarily, she was not and had not been pregnant (she was to die after childbirth a year later). No viewer could have known that. Gwen John's work at the same time was more conventional, and she did not paint herself nude. But in her *Girl Reading at the Window* (Cat. 15) she also painted a self-portrait, with a private sexual message, imagining herself seen through the eyes of her lover: the pose (as Susan Chitty observes, perhaps following one of the artist's letters) is the same as the one that she adopted when modelling for Rodin's sculpture, *The Muse* (Fig. 18). Modersohn-Becker's limited range, as she herself advised in her journal (1905, and repeated the following year), was for the sake of 'the intensity with which a subject is grasped, that is what makes for beauty in art.' This concentration was of course also the aim of Gwen John. The introspective sexuality of the *Sixth Wedding Anniversary* self-portrait, and of Modersohn-Becker's other references to birth and creation, led to her cultivation of subjects for the female beholder, in so far as they dealt with a woman's contemplation of herself as creator. There is of course no later work for comparison between the two artists, but Gwen was able to persist in her isolation, and seems also to have given a view of woman for a woman.

Gwen and Augustus could be grasped in a double biography, as if each were pursuing the prescribed roles of female and male. Contrary to superficial impressions, this would not be at all straightforward. Augustus's public personality, however much a stereotype, was not a reflection of his own wishes. Gwen was far more able to have charge of her own life; there were few occasions when she did anything against her will, and she was the more ruthless and dominating of the two. Her withdrawal to live and paint on her own, or in her own small circle, went further than a conventional limitation to minor genre and feminine subjects: it was a complete withdrawal from the group avant-garde position she could have comfortably occupied in London, and her solitariness was extreme.

Quinn considered that, with Marie Laurencin, 'You are the only two women

artists that I know in whose work I am interested, and I have constantly said . . . that you and she . . . paint like women and that most women artists try to paint like men and so they paint badly' (9 October 1920). There are features of Gwen John's work that are conventionally called feminine—the extreme delicacy of colouring, the fastidious application—but these are certainly not uniquely female, nor are they usefully so described when they might also apply, for example, to Seurat's work. Some elements bravely suggested as essentially feminine by Lucy Lippard, writing in 1973 about contemporary American work, are more plausibly relevant: a uniform density of surface, a central focus, a loose, parabolic outline. But these are necessarily vague and identified in the terms of much later abstract painting, and the lurking body image is inappropriate. Gwen John's response to her single subject of young women—and no one would doubt who it is that lives in her empty rooms—is remarkable. This is in part the triumph of her early debt to the little girls of Whistler's and of Steer's work of the 1890s. Her development was to this extent hermetic, and Rodin's drawing and sculpture, with which she was at one period so familiar, had little influence. In comparison to the late Whistler—and more so, to Steer—her models take on a curious interior personality that can only be described in human terms, and is paradoxically related to their inaction. They are exceptionally static, and only rarely does any feature, hand or nose, punctuate their outline. The studio in the mansard of the rue Terre Neuve at Meudon is a constant background. Fragments of Gwen John's own notes have been so often quoted as to be over-familiar, but on the subject of her own emotional strength, which maintained her standard of self criticism, there is naturally no other witness. She claimed an intention to 'put all that energy of loving into my drawing' when she finally lost Rodin. Her advice to Jeanne Foster, in about 1924, also recommended to her a transfer of mental activity to another person as a cure for depression, as if she had no doubt that such states could be deposited on another: 'To make it less difficult try and leave that part of you that

Fig. 18. Auguste Rodin's plaster model of Gwen John as *The Muse*, for the memorial to James McNeill Whistler. *c.*1906. Gelatin-silver print by Jacques-Ernest Bulloz. Paris, Musée Rodin.

Fig. 19. Photograph of Rodin, taken by Edward Steichen. 1907.

*The Cat*. Probably *c*.1905–8. Tate Gallery, London. Cat. 59.

*Black Cat on Blue and Pink*. Probably late 1910s to early 1920s. Ben John. Cat. 104.

suffers so and make another part of you go into somebody else's life—it doesn't matter whose life it is a child's even.' The cumulative impression, strongest at an exhibition, that the character of her models represented an ideal image to the artist, is supported by the care that she took to arrange them to a standard. Her most frequent models left no record, but when she was obliged by Quinn to paint Jeanne Foster, her sitter wrote back to him: 'She takes down my hair and does it like her own . . . she has me sit as she does, and I feel the absorption of her personality as I sit.' Some of her models sew, or hold a cloth, some read, one is in profile. Their room is spare, sometimes decorated with wild flowers. Although quietist, they are self-sufficient. She repeated one of her estimates of the value of her paintings: 'As to me, I cannot imagine why my vision will have some value in the world—and yet I know it will . . . I think it will count because I am patient and recieillé, in some degree' (undated letter, to Ursula Tyrwhitt). And in about 1924 she used the same word again to describe to Jeanne Foster a recommended quality: 'Yes, I think You give too much of your time to people: you ought to be more recieillé perhaps (don't you think that French word is beautiful—it means I think to gather in, to be collected).' Such an attitude she deliberately acquired in her life, and made evident in her figures.

A sense of the intensity of the image is achieved in each single painting, not just by the repetition of subject in different paintings (although she preferred her work to be seen in groups). John Rothenstein wrote of seeing Augustus John 'peer fixedly, almost obsessively, at pictures by Gwen, as though he could discern in them his own temperament in reverse'. What Augustus was thinking is conjecture, but the point is that he felt compelled to 'peer fixedly'. This is virtually a reflex response to Gwen John's work, as if its stillness were infectious. The later paintings are so even in tone that they have to be studied closely, and such staring is prolonged by the visual reward.

Gwen John's attendance at Quinn's dinner in Paris in 1923, with Brancusi and de Segonzac, is a surprise reminder that she belonged to the School of Paris (she had not sought the company, of course, and apparently declined the invitation next year from Mme. Braque). Her paintings of the 1920s are decidedly a move towards abstraction of the figure, in colour and detail, and in their monumental design. Yet their human character is so vital, and they are so unlike the stylishness of other painters in Paris, that it may be that a long-standing tradition of French painting was more important to her than current abstraction. There are only very few drawn studies for her later paintings as she usually painted directly, but the oils nevertheless have a quality of drawing comparable to paintings by, for example, Jean François Millet, in which shapes are summarized and balanced against each other. Gwen John's heavy areas of painted shadow on one side of her figures gives a massiveness like that of Millet's peasants, and this is the most French feature of her later paintings.

Her own gouaches, made in church after her conversion to Roman Catholicism in 1913, play upon her portrait style (Cat. 112–22). The extraordinary shapes which she worked so hard to find in the oil paintings were more readily visible in these gouaches, in the headdresses of the nuns and the disarray of chairbacks. In many instances the shapes are most eccentric. All of them are coloured exquisitely, and some are witty in caricature. She seems to have regarded the gouaches as an amusement, and enjoyed in the children portrayed an aspect of herself in which she cultivated the child. Despite the context of the church, these are less devotional in feeling than are her oil paintings.

The prayers which she copied and recopied, quoted by Augustus John after her

Fig. 21. Gwen John's house in rue Terre Neuve, Meudon. 1923. Michael Holroyd.

Fig. 20. Gwen John and John Quinn in Paris. 1923. Private collection.

death, along with other notes, show her preoccupation with her faith. It was only after 1926, however, that she was personally close to Jacques and Raïssa Maritain, the neo-Thomist theologians who lived near her in Meudon, and to Raïssa's sister Véra Oumançoff, and this was too late to affect her work. The compulsive repetition of her drawing was a habit already by 1907, when she drew a pair of cab horses at least twenty-seven times (all now preserved in the National Museum of Wales), and this was not any kind of devotional fetishism. The repetitions of the portrait of the seventeenth-century Abbess, Mère Poussepin (Cat. 17, 20), an obligation from the Convent at Meudon from about 1913, were the only paintings directly associated with her religion. She herself regarded them as the key to her later style, and she first used then what became later her typical three-quarter length pose, based in part on the engraved portrait she had to copy. Her involvement with the Church gave her the motivation to see through a task which must have been especially difficult, to complete so many paintings, none taken from life. After a period of little painting, when she might have ceased to work, these were a second start. The self-confidence required, then and later, she may well have found in her religion.

Gwen John had little admiration for the Cubist paintings collected by John Quinn. Her training, both at the Slade and with Whistler, had always been in the terms of the masters of the past, and the later portraits can be seen as a revision of her first attempts. The subjects are the same, and their recasting can be described

Gwen John

*Rue Terre Neuve, Meudon*. Probably late 1910s to early 1920s. Estate of the artist. Cat. 27.

(left) *Girl by a Window*. Probably c.1931. E. Pace Barnes. Cat. 52.

Fig. 22. Edwin John. *Gwen John's House at the Rue Babie, Meudon*. 1950s. Private collection.

as Post-Impressionist and more old-fashioned than 1920s developments. She probably did not know Clive Bell's book *Art*, published in 1914, in which he separates conventional painting, which he calls 'descriptive', from his admired 'Post-Impressionists'. His terms can be applied in essence, however, to the difference between Gwen John's work before and after the war, and this demonstrates the conservatism of her later style. Bell was writing of French and British artists who were followers of Cézanne. He did not come to terms with Cubism (only mentioned in a disapproving footnote), but praised an eloquent simplification of form. His prescription is mostly negative: avoid the narrative; avoid illusionism; avoid display of accomplishment; the subject should be difficult to see, so that lines and colours are more prominent. He recommends a reduction in scope—'severe limitations concentrate and intensify the artist's energies'. The positive and essential reward, for Bell, is his (inadequately explained) 'significant form'. Gwen John knew his sources and the artists he was promoting, and sometimes wrote in similar terms. An undated private note of hers (quoted by Mary Taubman, in the Arts Council exhibition catalogue, *Gwen John*, 1968) is titled 'The making of the portrait':

'1. the strange form
2. the pose and proportions
3. the atmosphere and notes
4. the finding of the forms'.

As with some other of her notes, it is impossible to understand precisely what she meant, but at the least this is far from a 'descriptive' approach to figure painting. Assuming that it refers to her own practice, it has to do with a method of design in which 'form' has the importance that it had for Clive Bell, even in its expressive character of 'strange'. Her colour notations are also a mix of methodical and personal, which it might eventually be possible some day to unravel.

Some of those who visited Gwen John's little house on the rue Babie in Meudon, where she lived from 1926, were shocked by what seemed appalling discomfort. This is certainly not how she viewed it herself. She bought the land, with its converted garage and its summerhouse, with money from sales at the 1926 exhibition, partly because it had a large garden, ideal for her cats. She must have thought it a self-indulgence: Meudon was a beautiful suburb, on high ground with views across Paris. Apart from the sketches of children in Brittany Gwen John's work is urban, and her models are essentially people who live in cities. In retiring to the rue Babie at the age of fifty she could satisfy a city dweller's love of nature. In the 1920s she admitted some satisfaction with her work, and was happy to show at the Salons and at her retrospective exhibition in London. Having set and maintained her own standards in painting there was no pressure for variety, and the narrow range allowed the expression to be the more powerful.

Few artists reveal a greater commitment than Gwen John. The paintings are beautiful and yet also challenging and uncomfortable. They work like a persistent force on their subject, and when the excitements of changes of style are no longer an issue or a surprise, the way in which she has dealt with the figure remains a profound example of the communication of inner feeling.

*Girl with a Blue Scarf*. Probably c.1923–4. Museum of Modern Art, New York. Cat. 48.

*Woman with Hands Crossed*. Probably *c*.1923–4. Carter Burden. Cat. 47.

(top left) *Portrait of Winifred John*. Sheffield City Art Galleries. Cat. 55.

(top right) *Winifred John in a Large Hat*. National Museum of Wales, Cardiff. Cat. 53.

(below left) *A Woman Asleep on a Sofa*. Private collection. Cat. 54.

(right) *Seated Girl with Hat (Winifred John)*. Private collection. Cat. 56.

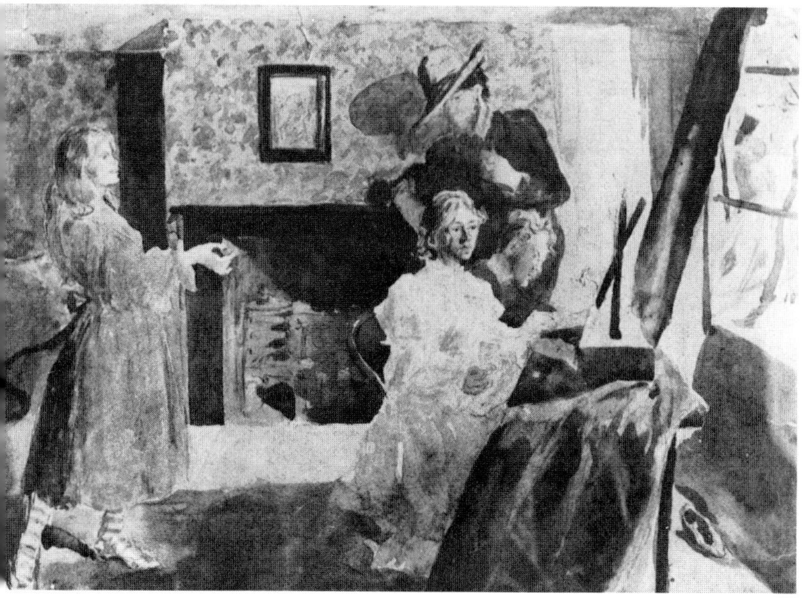

(above left) *Portrait Group*. Private collection. Cat. 57.

(above) *Self-Portrait*. National Portrait Gallery, London. Cat. 5.

*Interior with Figures*. National Gallery of Victoria, Melbourne. Cat. 3.

*Portrait of Mrs Atkinson*. Probably c.1897–8. Metropolitan Museum of Art, New York. Cat. 2.

(right) *Portrait of the Artist's Sister Winifred*. Probably c.1897–8. Private collection. Cat. 1.

(right) *The Artist in her Room in Paris*. Private collection. Cat. 11.

(far right) *Self-Portrait Holding a Letter*. Musée Rodin, Paris. Cat. 67.

(below right) *La Chambre sur la Cour*. Helena D. Henderson. Cat. 9.

(below far right) *Woman Dressing*. Howard Kopet. Cat. 63.

(far left) *Female Nude Standing, Right Hand on Hip*. National Museum of Wales, Cardiff. Cat. 64.

(left) *Self-Portrait, Naked, Sitting on a Bed*. Private collection. Cat. 66.

*Portrait of Dorelia at Toulouse*. British Museum, London. Cat. 58.

*Nude Girl*. c.1909–10.
Tate Gallery, London.
Cat. 12.

(right) *Dorelia in a Black Dress*. 1903–4. Tate Gallery, London. Cat. 7.

*Head of a Lady*. Private collection. Cat. 72.

(far right) *Head of a Young Woman*. Yale University Art Gallery. Cat. 68.

(below) *Portrait of a Lady, Half-Length, Leaning Back*. Private collection. Cat. 69.

(below centre) *Portrait of a Lady*. Borough of Thamesdown Museums and Art Gallery. Cat. 70.

(below right) *Portrait of a Lady*. Private collection, London. Cat. 71.

*Chloe Boughton-Leigh.* Tate Gallery, London. Cat. 8.

*Girl with Bare Shoulders.* Museum of Modern Art, New York. Cat. 13.

*Portrait of Mère Poussepin*. Probably late 1910s. Southampton Art Gallery. Cat. 20.

*The Nun*. Probably mid 1910s. National Gallery of Victoria, Melbourne. Cat. 18.

(right) *Bust of a Woman*. Albright-Knox Art Gallery, Buffalo. Cat. 74.

(far right) *Étude pour 'Les Suppliantes'*. Private collection. Cat. 73.

*Sketch of a Seated Cat*. Victoria and Albert Museum, London. Cat. 61.

(below) *Cat*. Tate Gallery, London. Cat. 62.

(bottom left) *Study of a Tortoise-Shell Cat*. Private collection. Cat. 60.

(right) *Portrait of a Young Nun*. Private collection. Cat. 21.

(far right) *Mère Poussepin*. Private collection. Cat. 17.

*Little Girl in Check Coat with Woman in Black*. Probably 1920s. Private collection. Cat. 119.

*A Nun and Two Girls in Church*. Probably 1920s. Private collection. Cat. 116.

*Little Girl with a Large Hat and Straw-Coloured Hair*. Probably late 1910s. Private collection. Cat. 89.

*Petit Profil*. Probably 1920s. Mimi and Sanford Feld. Cat. 118.

*Woman and Child in a Railway Carriage*. Private collection. Cat. 75.

(above right) *Profile of a Bourgeois Couple*. Howard Kopet. Cat. 76.

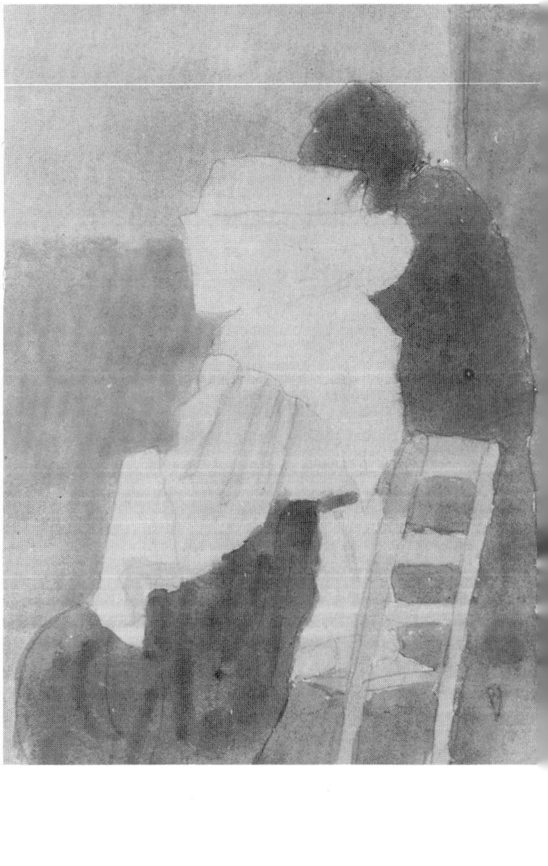

*Young Woman in a Hat*. Stanford University Museum of Art. Cat. 79.

(far right) *Seated Nun and Standing Woman in Church*. Private collection. Cat. 78.

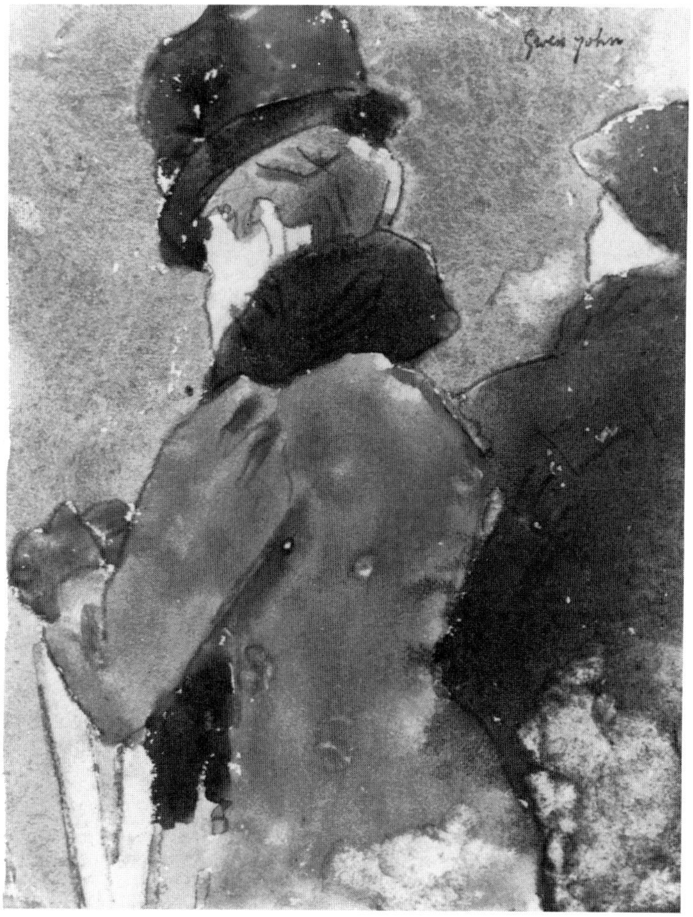

(above left) *Back View of a Soldier, Standing, in Conversation with a Girl*. Carter Burden. Cat. 77.

*Mademoiselle Pouvereau*. Private collection, San Francisco. Cat. 88.

(far left) *Girl Praying, Back View*. Stanford University Museum of Art. Cat. 81.

*Little Fair-Haired Boy Standing in Church*. Carter Burden. Cat. 80.

*Seated Girl*. Private collection. Cat. 83.

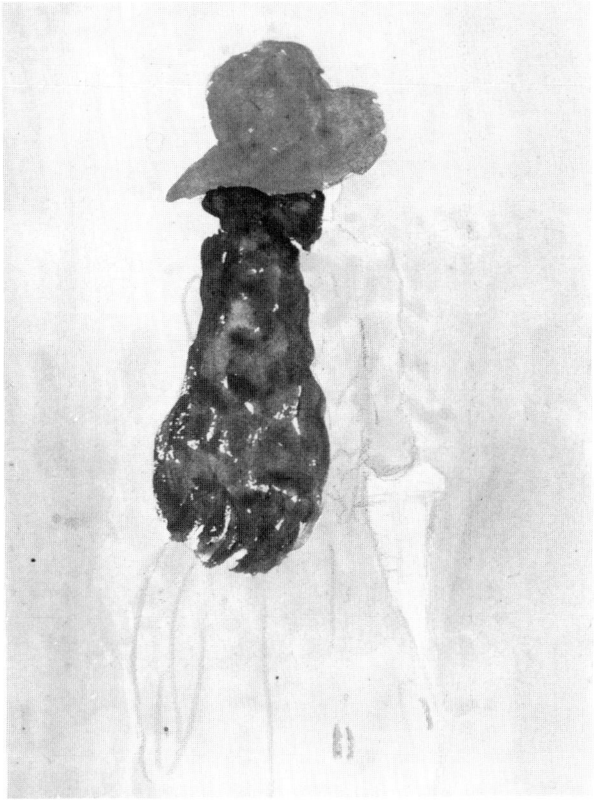

*A Girl with Long Hair Kneeling in Church, Seen from Behind*. National Museum of Wales, Cardiff. Cat. 115.

*Two Women in Church*. Mrs Martha Hare. Cat. 82.

*Seated Woman, Dressed in Black*. Carter Burden. Cat. 86.

*Young Girl in Hooded Cloak*. Private collection. Cat. 87.

*A Girl and an Older Woman in Church*. Private collection. Cat. 85.

(below) *A Nun and Two Girls in Church*. Private collection. Cat. 84.

*A Girl Wearing a Hat and Coat with a Fur Collar, Seated in Church*. National Museum of Wales, Cardiff. Cat. 117.

*A Rag Doll*. Private collection. Cat. 97.

*Girl with Plaits and a High-Crowned Hat*. Duke of Devonshire. Cat. 99.

*Marie Hamonet with Arms Crossed*. Private collection. Cat. 102.

*Louise Gautier Wearing a Cape*. Private collection. Cat. 98.

*Elisabeth de Willman Grabowska*. Victoria and Albert Museum, London. Cat. 96.

(below) *Child Posing*. Private collection. Cat. 100.

*Girl with Hands in her Lap*. Fitzwilliam Museum, Cambridge. Cat. 101.

*Breton Boy*. Private collection. Cat. 92.

(below) *Three-Quarter-Length of a Young Woman with High Cheekbones*. Cecil Higgins Art Gallery, Bedford. Cat. 94.

*The Child with a Polo*. Private collection. Cat. 95.

*Seated Girl Holding a Child.* Private collection. Cat. 122.

(below left) *Seated Girl with Folded Arms.* Private collection. Cat. 93.

*Profile of Arthur Symons.* E. Pace Barnes. Cat. 103.

(top left) *La Petite Modèle*. Private collection. Cat. 23.

(top right) *Girl in Rose*. Private collection. Cat. 24.

(below left) *A Corner of the Artist's Room, Rue Terre Neuve*. Private collection. Cat. 90.

*Woman Holding a Flower*. Birmingham City Museum and Art Gallery. Cat. 26.

*Young Woman Holding a Black Cat*. Tate Gallery, London. Cat. 29.

(below) *Girl Holding a Cat*. Private collection. Cat. 105.

(far left) *Study of a Young Girl*. Hugh Lane Municipal Gallery of Modern Art, Dublin. Cat. 32.

*Girl Holding a Cat*. Paul Mellon Collection, Upperville, Virginia. Cat. 30.

*Seated Girl with Sewing*. Mrs R. Pilkington. Cat. 33.

(far right) *Seated Woman Wearing a Blue Bow*. Private collection. Cat. 37.

(below) *Girl in a Green Dress*. National Museum of Wales, Cardiff. Cat. 38.

*Woman with Cloak*. Albright-Knox Art Gallery, Buffalo. Cat. 41.

*Girl in Blue*. Private collection. Cat. 34.

*Young Woman in a Red Shawl*. Private collection. Cat. 40.

*Portrait of a Young Woman Wearing a Locket*. Ben John. Cat. 36.

*Girl in a Blue Dress*. Private collection. Cat. 16.

(above right) *The Letter*. Manchester City Art Galleries. Cat. 43.

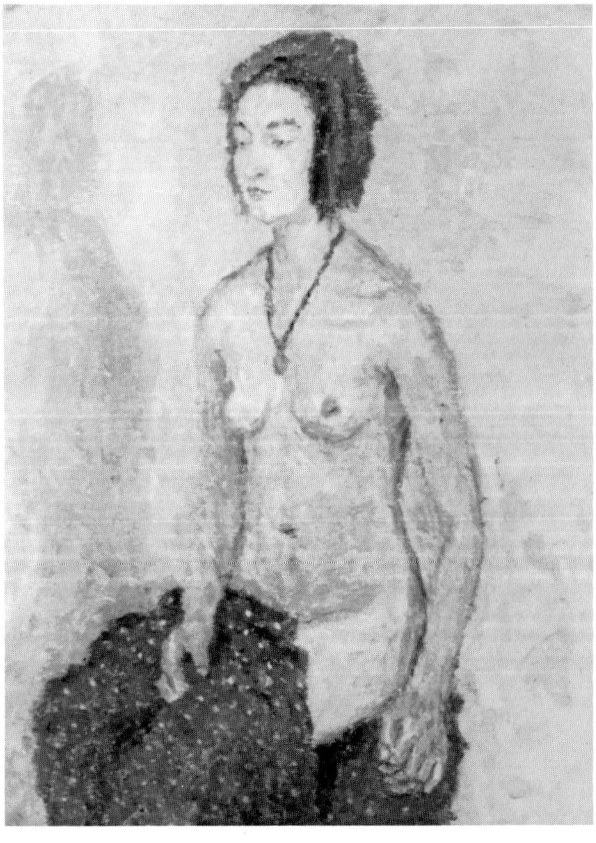

*Seated Nude*. Private collection. Cat. 46.

ɔrtrait of Miss Bridget Sarah Bishop. Estate of the artist. Cat. 50.

*Young Woman Wearing a Large Hat*. Paul Mellon Collection, Upperville, Virginia. Cat. 39.

*At Meudon*. Whitworth Art Gallery, University of Manchester. Cat. 106.

(below) *Trees*. National Museum of Wales, Cardiff. Cat. 125.

*Still Life with a Vase of Flowers and an Inkwell*. Private collection. Cat. 49.

(far left) *Flowers and Brown Bowl*. Carter Burden. Cat. 109.

*Ivy Leaves in a White Jug*. National Museum of Wales, Cardiff. Cat. 110.

(far left) *Flowers in Jug*. Private collection. Cat. 124.

*A Vase of Flowers, with Colour Notes*. National Museum of Wales, Cardiff. Cat. 108.

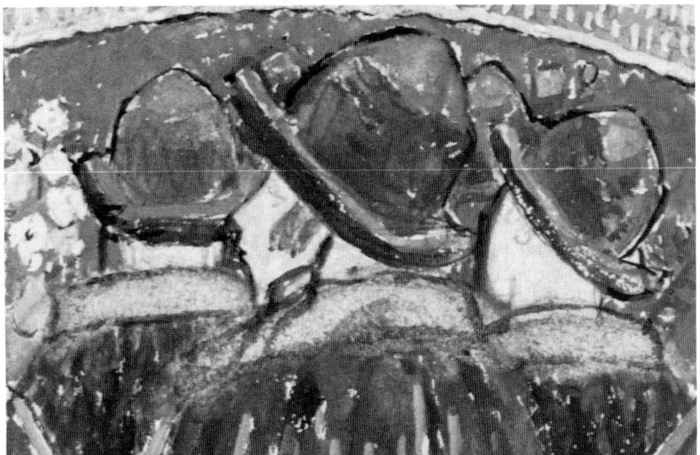

(top left) *Two Girls Kneeling in Church*. Private collection. Cat. 113.

(top right) *Woman and Two Nuns in Church*. Mrs Martha Hare. Cat. 114.

(below left) *Les Chapeaux à Brides*, Mimi and Sanford Feld. Cat. 120.

*Woman in a Railway Carriage*. Private collection. Cat. 123.

(above left) *The Victorian Sisters.* Private collection. Cat. 121.

*Two Girls in Church.* Mrs Martha Hare. Cat. 112.

*Head of Seated Girl in Church, Seen from Behind*, two drawings from a set of six. National Museum of Wales, Cardiff. Cat. 126.

# Catalogue

CECILY LANGDALE

Catalogue entries for Cat. 111, 125 and 126 have been provided by David Fraser Jenkins.

Certain works will not be exhibited in all three locations of London, Manchester and New Haven. These are: Cat. 12, 21, 29, 94 (London only); Cat. 14 (London and Manchester only); Cat. 17, 47, 68, 69, 77, 80, 86, 109 (New Haven only).

Exhibitions and published references that occurred during the artist's lifetime are mentioned in the catalogue under EXHIBITED and LITERATURE; 'Langdale' refers to Cecily Langdale's forthcoming *Gwen John: A Catalogue Raisonné of the Paintings and a Selection of the Drawings*, which gives further references and complete provenances. For explanation of other abbreviations, see under Selected Exhibitions, Galleries and Sales and Selected Bibliography, p. 93.

Page numbers given after the dates of works refer to illustrations (an asterisk denotes a colour plate).

1. *Portrait of the Artist's Sister Winifred*. Probably c.1897–8. (p. 51*)

Private collection

Oil on canvas, 18 × 16 in. (45.7 × 40.6 cm.)

PROVENANCE: the artist, until c.1901; Louise Salaman (Mrs E. W.) Bishop, c.1901; by descent to present owner

EXHIBITED: NEAC, *26th Exhibition*, 1901, no. 102; Chenil, 1926, no. 43

LITERATURE: M. Chamot, 'An Undiscovered Artist: Gwen John', *Country Life*, 19 June 1926, p. 885; Langdale, no. 4

The model is the artist's younger sister. In 1897–8, while at the Slade, Gwen and Augustus John shared rooms at 21 Fitzroy Street. They were joined there by Winifred, who had come to London in order to study the violin. This portrait was probably painted then.

Louise Salaman Bishop, the first owner of the picture, was a friend and fellow-student of Gwen John at the Slade.

2. *Portrait of Mrs Atkinson*. Probably c.1897–8. (p. 50*)

New York, Metropolitan Museum of Art

Oil on composition board, $11\frac{7}{8} \times 13\frac{3}{4}$ in. (30.2 × 34.9 cm.)

PROVENANCE: Michel Salaman; Arthur Tooth and Sons Ltd., London, until 1951; Mary Cushing (Mrs James) Fosburgh; bequeathed by her to Metropolitan Museum of Art, 1978

EXHIBITED: NEAC, *25th Exhibition*, 1900, no. 38; Chenil, 1926, no. 35

LITERATURE: Chamot, p. 884; Langdale, no. 6

The sitter's identity is unknown. The picture was probably painted in London; the room may well be that in *Portrait Group* (Cat. 57) and in Augustus John's drawing of his sister of about 1897 (Fig. 1).

3. *Interior with Figures*. Probably c.1898–9. (p. 49)

Melbourne, National Gallery of Victoria

Oil on canvas, $18\frac{1}{8} \times 13\frac{1}{8}$ in. (46 × 33.4 cm.)

PROVENANCE: Mr and Mrs C. H. Collins Baker, Pasadena, California; presented by Mrs C. H. Collins Baker to the National Gallery of Victoria, 1947

EXHIBITED: ? NEAC, *27th Exhibition*, 1902, no. 95; ? Carfax, 1903, no. 6

LITERATURE: Langdale, no. 7

The figure at the left is the artist herself and that at the right is Ida Nettleship, who was to marry Augustus John in 1901. It is the only known portrait of Ida by Gwen John.

Gwen and Ida met at the Slade and in the autumn of 1897 went to Paris together, along with Gwen Salmond, to study art. Architectural details suggest that this interior is French rather than English; it is probably a room at 12 rue Froidevaux, where the three young women lived while they were studying in Paris.

The early history of *Interior with Figures* is not known. Its first owner, C. H. Collins Baker, had Slade connections and was Secretary of the New English Art Club. If this is the picture shown in 1902 or 1903, he may well have acquired it then.

4. *Self-Portrait in a Red Blouse*. c.1900. (frontispiece*)

London, The Trustees of the Tate Gallery

Oil on canvas, $17\frac{5}{8} \times 13\frac{3}{4}$ in. (44.8 × 35 cm.). Signed in monogram at lower right: *GMJ*.

PROVENANCE: Professor Frederick Brown; Miss Ellen Brown; purchased by the Tate Gallery, 1942

EXHIBITED: ? NEAC, *24th Exhibition*, 1900, no. 104; NEAC, London, 1925, no. 65; NEAC, Manchester, 1925, no. 304; Secession, Vienna, *Meisterwerke Englischer Malerei aus Drei Jahrhunderten*, 1927, no. 157; Palais des Beaux-Arts de Bruxelles, *Exposition de Peinture Anglaise Moderne*, 1929, no. 109

LITERATURE: Langdale, no. 8

In a photograph of 1902, Gwen John appears very much as she does here: her hair is arranged in the same fashion, and she wears the same earrings and cameo and ribbon.

*Self-Portrait in a Red Blouse* is the only known painting signed by the artist on the recto. Fred Brown, the first owner, taught Gwen John at the Slade. In his own self-portrait (Ferens Art Gallery, Kingston upon Hull), Brown stands before a wall on which this picture hangs.

5. *Self-Portrait*. Probably c.1900–3. (p. 49)

London, National Portrait Gallery

Oil on canvas, $24 \times 14\frac{7}{8}$ in. (61 × 37.7 cm.)

PROVENANCE: the artist; Augustus John, until 1961; Dorothy (Dorelia) McNeill (Mrs Augustus John); purchased from her by the National Art Collections Fund and presented to the National Portrait Gallery to mark Sir Alec Martin's forty years of devoted service to the Fund, 1965

LITERATURE: Langdale, no. 9

6. *The Student*. 1903–4. (p. 10*)

Manchester City Art Galleries

Oil on canvas, $22\frac{1}{8} \times 13$ in. (56.1 × 33 cm.)

PROVENANCE: the artist; Charles L. Rutherston, probably from 1909; donated by him to the City of Manchester Art Gallery, 1925

EXHIBITED: NEAC, *42nd Exhibition*, 1909, no. 51; NEAC, London, 1925, no. 29; NEAC, Manchester, 1925, no. 301

LITERATURE: Langdale, no. 11

The model is Dorothy (Dorelia) McNeill, the subject of three other paintings (see Cat. 7) and various drawings (see

Cat. 58) by Gwen John, and of countless portraits by Augustus John. She and Gwen met in 1902 or 1903, and in August 1903 set out on a walking tour to Rome. They never arrived in Italy, but spent the winter of 1903–4 in Toulouse, where this picture was painted.

Charles Rutherston, the first owner, was the brother of Gwen John's artist friend William Rothenstein and himself a collector. He owned four paintings by Gwen John (Cat. 22, 43, and 44).

7. *Dorelia in a Black Dress*. 1903–4. (p. 55*)
London, The Trustees of the Tate Gallery
Oil on canvas, $28\frac{3}{4} \times 19\frac{1}{4}$ in. (73 × 48.9 cm.)
PROVENANCE: the artist; Mrs Ursula Tyrwhitt; via New Chenil Galleries, to the Duveen Paintings Fund, 1926; presented by the Fund to the Tate Gallery, 1949
EXHIBITED: Chenil, 1926, no. 44; Secession, Vienna, *Meisterwerke Englischer Malerei aus Drei Jahrhunderten*, 1927, no. 159
LITERATURE: Chamot, pp. 884–5, illus.; Langdale, no. 12
See note to Cat. 6 (*The Student*).

8. *Chloe Boughton-Leigh*. *c*.1907. (p. 57)
London, The Trustees of the Tate Gallery
Oil on canvas, 23 × 15 in. (58.4 × 38.1 cm.)
PROVENANCE: the artist, until 1908; via NEAC, to Ellen Theodosia (Chloe) Boughton-Leigh, until 1925; via NEAC, to the Tate Gallery, 1925
EXHIBITED: NEAC, *40th Exhibition*, 1908, no. 78; NEAC, London, 1925, no. 76; NEAC, Manchester, 1925, no. 303; Chenil, 1926, probably no. 18; ? National Eisteddfod, Fishguard, *Exhibition of Contemporary Welsh Art*, 1936
LITERATURE: Chamot, illus. p. 885; Alfred H. Barr, Jr., 'Modern Art in London Museums', *The Arts*, vol. XIV, no. 4, October 1928, p. 190, illus. p. 194; Sir Joseph Duveen, *Thirty Years of British Art*, 1930, illus. p. 109; *Tate Gallery Illustrations, British School*, 1938, illus. p. 101; Langdale, no. 14

This is the earliest of three known paintings of Ellen Theodosia (Chloe) Boughton-Leigh (see Cat. 14 and 26). Gwen met Chloe and her artist sister Maude in Paris, and formed a lifelong friendship with them. The picture is painted on a canvas $22\frac{1}{4}$ in. (56.5 cm.) high, to which the artist has added a strip of wood at the bottom.

9. *La Chambre sur la Cour*. *c*.1907–8. (p. 53)
Collection of Helena D. Henderson
Oil on canvas, $12\frac{1}{2} \times 8\frac{1}{2}$ in. (31.8 × 21.6 cm.)
PROVENANCE: the artist, until 1908; via NEAC, to Mrs Frances Cornford
EXHIBITED: NEAC, *40th Exhibition*, 1908, no. 109; NEAC, London, 1925, no. 79; NEAC, Manchester, 1925, no. 300
LITERATURE: Langdale, no. 15

*La Chambre sur la Cour* is the first of four oil self-portraits in a Parisian room (see Cat. 11 and 15). The same room is probably the setting for Cat. 15, in which the figure is identically attired, and for *A Lady Reading* (Tate Gallery, London). The wicker chair reappears frequently in Gwen John's paintings (see Cat. 10, 15, 42 and 43), and the tortoise-shell cat, the artist's adored companion until 1908, is the subject of many drawings (see Cat. 59–62).

10. *A Corner of the Artist's Room in Paris*. 1907–9. (p. 31*)
Sheffield City Art Galleries
Oil on canvas, $12\frac{1}{2} \times 10\frac{1}{2}$ in. (31.7 × 26.7 cm.)
PROVENANCE: estate of the artist (P.J.1); Dorothy (Dorelia) McNeill (Mrs Augustus John), as of 1952; presented by her to the Sheffield City Art Galleries, 1964
LITERATURE: Langdale, no. 16
See note to Cat. 9 (*La Chambre sur la Cour*).

In a variant of the composition (private collection), the window stands open to reveal the buildings across the street. The setting is 87 rue du Cherche-Midi, on the top floor of which the artist lived from 1907 until 1909.

11. *The Artist in her Room in Paris*. 1907–9. (p. 53)
Private collection
Oil on canvas, $10\frac{3}{4} \times 9$ in. (27.3 × 22.9 cm.)
PROVENANCE: the artist; Augustus John, until 1961; by descent to present owner
LITERATURE: Langdale, no. 18
See note to Cat. 10 (*A Corner of the Artist's Room in Paris*).

Several related self-portrait drawings (for example, Cat. 66) are set in the same corner of the artist's rue du Cherche-Midi room. In *Self-Portrait* (Cat. 65), her appearance is very much as it is here.

12. *Nude Girl*. *c*.1909–10. (p. 54*)
London, The Trustees of the Tate Gallery
Oil on canvas, $17\frac{1}{2} \times 11$ in. (44.5 × 28 cm.)
PROVENANCE: the artist; presented to the Contemporary Art Society by an anonymous member, 1911; presented to the Tate Gallery by the Society, 1917
EXHIBITED: ? NEAC, *43rd Exhibition*, 1910, no. 230; Manchester, *Contemporary Art Society Loan Exhibition*, 1911, no. 225; Goupil Gallery, London, *First Public Exhibition in London*, 1913, no. 66; Contemporary Art Society, London, *Purchases and Gifts*, 1914, no. 9; Contemporary Art Society, Belfast, *Modern Paintings*, 1914, no. 7
LITERATURE: Barr, p. 190; Langdale, no. 19

Fenella Lovell, a Paris acquaintance of the artist, posed for *Nude Girl* and for a variant in which she wears a white dress (Cat. 13). Gwen John disliked her model, whom she thought had a 'horrid character', and was relieved when the paintings were completed. One of the two pictures (and possibly both) was exhibited at the New English Art Club in 1910.

13. *Girl with Bare Shoulders*. *c*.1909–10. (p. 57)
New York, The Museum of Modern Art
Oil on canvas, $17\frac{1}{8} \times 10\frac{1}{4}$ in. (43.5 × 26 cm.)
PROVENANCE: estate of the artist (P.J.12), until 1946; M. Georges Wildenstein, London, until 1958
EXHIBITED: ? NEAC, *43rd Exhibition*, 1910, no. 230
LITERATURE: Langdale, no. 20
See note to Cat. 12 (*Nude Girl*).

14. *Chloe Boughton-Leigh*. 1910. (p. 11*)
Leeds City Art Galleries
Oil on canvas, $23\frac{3}{4} \times 15$ in. (60.3 × 38.1 cm.)
PROVENANCE: the artist, until 1914; John Quinn, until 1924; John Quinn estate, until 1927; American Art Galleries, 1927, lot 344; J. P. Lucas; Ellen Theodosia (Chloe) Boughton-Leigh, until 1947; Mrs Sylvia Molloy, until 1955; via Matthiesen, to Leeds City Art Galleries
EXHIBITED: The Sculptors' Gallery, New York, *Seven English Modernists*, 1922; Art Center, 1926, no. 69
LITERATURE: John Quinn ledger, pp. 117, 176; *John Quinn Collection*, p. 18, illus. p. 147; Langdale, no. 21
See note to Cat. 8 (*Chloe Boughton-Leigh*).

There is a fragmentary sketch of the same figure on the verso. The artist began, and probably essentially completed, the painting during the autumn of 1910, although she may have continued to work on it as late as the summer of 1914, when she sent it to John Quinn, along with two related drawings of the sitter (Cat. 73 and 74).

John Quinn, the distinguished American attorney and collector, was Gwen John's patron from 1910 until his death in 1924; the years of his patronage were those of her greatest artistic productivity. Quinn purchased almost every picture that she sold during that time, acquiring a considerable collection of her work (see Cat. 15, 17, 23, 24, 34, 41, 46–8, 73, 74, 79, 81, 83 and 87).

15. *Girl Reading at the Window*. 1911. (p. 6*)

New York, The Museum of Modern Art

Oil on canvas, 16 × 10 in. (40.6 × 25.4 cm.)

PROVENANCE: the artist, until *c*. December 1912; John Quinn, until 1924; John Quinn estate, until 1927; American Art Galleries, 1927, lot 465; Julia Quinn Anderson (sister of John Quinn), until 1934; Mary Anderson (Mrs Thomas F.) Conroy (her daughter), until 1970; bequeathed by her to The Museum of Modern Art, 1971

EXHIBITED: NEAC, *46th Exhibition*, 1911, no. 58; Armory of the Sixty-Ninth Regiment, New York, Art Institute of Chicago, and Copley Hall, Copley Society of Boston, *International Exhibition of Modern Art*, 1913, no. 578; The Sculptors' Gallery, New York, *Seven English Modernists*, 1922; Art Center, 1926, no. 72

LITERATURE: John Quinn ledger, pp. 117, 176; *John Quinn Collection*, p. 18, illus. p. 149; Langdale, no. 25

See note to Cat. 9 (*La Chambre sur la Cour*).

*Girl Reading at the Window* was the first work by Gwen John to enter John Quinn's collection. She completed the painting in August 1911, but when she began it is unknown. It is very close in manner to *La Chambre sur la Cour* of several years earlier; the figure, again a self-portrait, is attired identically and poses in what appears to be the same room.

16. *Girl in a Blue Dress*. Probably *c*.1914–15. (p. 76)

Private collection

Oil on canvas, $16\frac{1}{2}$ × 12 in. (41.9 × 30.5 cm.) (sight)

PROVENANCE: private collection, probably as of the 1940s; by descent to present owner

LITERATURE: Langdale, no. 27

This belongs to the earliest and one of the largest series of paintings in Gwen John's *oeuvre*; there are seven located versions of the composition, which differ one from the other only in detail. A variant (private collection) is known to have been completed before March 1916, when it was received in New York by John Quinn.

The sitter is unidentified; according to the artist, she was 'just a neighbour' in Meudon. She was the model most frequently used by Gwen John, and is called 'the Convalescent' after a later group of pictures for which she posed (see Cat. 42 and 43).

17. *Mère Poussepin*. *c*.1913–20. (p. 61)

Private collection

Oil on canvas, $34\frac{1}{2}$ × 26 in. (87.6 × 66 cm.)

PROVENANCE: the artist; Convent of the Soeurs de Charité Dominicaines de la Présentation de la Sainte Vierge de Tours, Meudon, until 1921; John Quinn, until 1924; Julia Quinn Anderson (sister of John Quinn), until 1934; Mary Anderson (Mrs Thomas F.) Conroy (her daughter), until 1970

EXHIBITED: ? Société du Salon d'Automne, Paris, 1919, no. 976; The Sculptors' Gallery, New York, *Seven English Modernists*, 1922

LITERATURE: John Quinn account book, p. 57; *John Quinn Collection*, p. 18; Langdale, no. 37

There are six known portraits of Mère Marie Poussepin (1653–1744), founder in 1696 of the Soeurs de Charité Dominicaines de la Présentation de la Sainte Vierge de Tours. They were commissioned from Gwen John in about 1913 by the Meudon chapter of that order.

This canvas, begun by 1913, is the first of the series, and is the only one ever actually owned by the Meudon convent, where it was hanging by early 1920.

It is likely that the artist worked on several versions concurrently. The composition is based upon a 1911 prayer card of Mère Poussepin (based, in turn, upon a contemporary portrait of the Foundress). Three of the series, including this picture, follow that prayer card closely; the others (see Cat. 20), which are probably slightly later, are simpler in composition.

John Quinn's companion Jeanne Robert Foster saw this painting at the Meudon convent in 1920, and recommended that the collector attempt to buy it; he did so the following year.

18. *The Nun*. Probably mid 1910s. (p. 59*)

Melbourne, National Gallery of Victoria

Oil on cardboard, 28 × $20\frac{1}{2}$ in. (71.2 × 52 cm.)

PROVENANCE: estate of the artist (P.J.30), until 1946; via Matthiesen, to Professor Schwabe, London; National Gallery of Victoria, Felton Bequest, 1947

LITERATURE: Langdale, no. 40

The subject surely was a nun of the Meudon chapter of the Soeurs de Charité Dominicaines de la Présentation de la Sainte Vierge de Tours; another portrait of her (private collection) bears the old title *Soeur Marie Céline*.

The composition of *The Nun* is the same as that of *Mère Poussepin* (Cat. 17), and the two pictures date from much the same time. The habit of that Dominican order remained essentially unchanged for more than two hundred years, except for the headpiece, which altered radically. Curiously, this twentieth-century nun wears the seventeenth-century cornette rather than that of her own day (see Cat. 78).

19. *The Teapot (Interior: Second Version)*. *c*.1915–16. (p. 19*)

Yale University Art Gallery

Oil on canvas, $13\frac{1}{8}$ × $9\frac{1}{2}$ in. (33.3 × 24.1 cm.)

PROVENANCE: estate of the artist (P.J.49), until 1949; via Matthiesen, to Mr and Mrs James Fosburgh, New York; given by them to Yale University Art Gallery, 1978

LITERATURE: Langdale, no. 50

Another version of the composition (Cleveland Museum of Art) belonged to John Quinn, who received it from the artist in March 1916. The round table and the teapot reappear frequently in later paintings (see Cat. 42–4).

20. *Portrait of Mère Poussepin*. Probably late 1910s. (p. 58*)

Southampton Art Gallery

Oil on canvas, 27 × $20\frac{1}{8}$ in. (68.7 × 51.2 cm.)

PROVENANCE: estate of the artist (P.J.59), until 1954; via Matthiesen, to Southampton Art Gallery, 1954

LITERATURE: Langdale, no. 54

See note to Cat. 17 (*Mère Poussepin*).

21. *Portrait of a Young Nun*. Probably late 1910s. (p. 61)

Private collection

Oil on canvas, $23\frac{3}{4}$ × $15\frac{3}{4}$ in. (60.3 × 40 cm.)

PROVENANCE: estate of the artist (P.J.31), until 1982; via d'Offay, to private collection

LITERATURE: Langdale, no. 56

Like the slightly older *religieuse* of Cat. 18, this nun undoubtedly belonged to the Meudon chapter of the Soeurs de Charité Dominicaines de la Présentation de la Sainte Vierge de Tours; and, like that woman, she wears the headpiece of Mère Poussepin's day rather than her own. The composition of the picture is identical to that of *Portrait of Mère Poussepin* (Cat. 20).

22. *Flowers*. Probably late 1910s. (p. 22*)

Manchester City Art Galleries

Oil on canvas, $13\frac{7}{8}$ × $10\frac{3}{4}$ in. (35.2 × 27.2 cm.)

PROVENANCE: Charles L. Rutherston, until 1927; Mrs Charles L. Rutherston and Miss Rutherston, 1927; given by them to the City of Manchester Art Gallery, 1928

EXHIBITED: ? Chenil, 1926, no. 20

LITERATURE: Langdale, no. 59

The round table reappears with different still-life arrangements in *La Petite Modèle* (Cat. 23) and *Girl in Rose* (Cat. 24); the object in the background is probably the bookcase of Cat. 24.

In 1926, Charles Rutherston presented his collection, which included three works by Gwen John (Cat. 6, 43 and 44), to the City of Manchester Art Gallery. Because *Flowers* was not among them, it may be assumed that he acquired it at a later date.

23. *La Petite Modèle*. Probably late 1910s. (p. 72)
Private collection
Oil on canvas, $21\frac{1}{2} \times 18$ in. (54.6 × 45.7 cm.)
PROVENANCE: the artist; John Quinn, until 1924; John Quinn estate, until 1927; American Art Galleries, 1927, lot 338; Julia Quinn Anderson (sister of John Quinn), until 1934; Mary Anderson (Mrs Thomas F.) Conroy (her daughter) until 1970; private collection, until 1982
EXHIBITED: ? Société du Salon d'Automne, Paris, 1923
LITERATURE: *John Quinn Collection*, p. 18; Langdale, no. 61

The identity of the young blonde model is unknown; she also sat for *Girl in Rose* (Cat. 24), *Girl in Profile* (Cat. 25) and *Little Girl with Large Hat and Straw-Coloured Hair* (Cat. 89).

John Quinn acquired *La Petite Modèle* sometime after March 1922, when he lent all his works by Gwen John to the Sculptors' Gallery exhibition *Seven English Modernists*; this picture was not among them.

24. *Girl in Rose*. Probably late 1910s. (p. 72)
Private collection
Oil on canvas, $18\frac{1}{4} \times 14\frac{1}{4}$ in. (46.3 × 36.2 cm.)
PROVENANCE: the artist, until 1924; John Quinn estate, until at least 1926; Julia Quinn Anderson (sister of John Quinn), until 1934; Mary Anderson (Mrs Thomas F.) Conroy (her daughter), until 1970
EXHIBITED: Salon des Tuileries, Paris, 1924, no. 786
LITERATURE: *John Quinn Collection*, p. 18; Langdale, no. 64

See note to Cat. 23 (*La Petite Modèle*).

25. *Girl in Profile*. Probably late 1910s. (p. 23*)
Cardiff, National Museum of Wales
Oil on canvas, $18 \times 12\frac{1}{2}$ in. (45.7 × 31.7 cm.)
PROVENANCE: estate of the artist (no estate number given), until 1940; National Museum of Wales, gift of the Contemporary Art Society for Wales
LITERATURE: Langdale, no. 65

See note to Cat. 23 (*La Petite Modèle*).

26. *Woman Holding a Flower*. Probably late 1910s to early 1920s. (p. 72)
Birmingham City Museum and Art Gallery
Oil on canvas, $17\frac{5}{8} \times 11\frac{1}{2}$ in. (44.7 × 29.2 cm.)
PROVENANCE: Clifford Hall; Roland, Browse, and Delbanco, London, as of 1949; purchased by the Friends of the Art Gallery, Birmingham Museums and Art Gallery, 1949
LITERATURE: Langdale, no. 67

See note to Cat. 8 (*Chloe Boughton-Leigh*).

This is the last of the three known paintings of Ellen Theodosia (Chloe) Boughton-Leigh (see Cat. 8 and 14). The early history of *Woman Holding a Flower* is unclear. However, John Quinn owned two oils of the sitter, one of which is Cat. 14; the other is probably this picture.

27. *Rue Terre Neuve, Meudon*. Probably late 1910s to early 1920s. (p. 43*)
Estate of the artist (P.J.102)
Oil on canvas, $8\frac{3}{4} \times 10\frac{7}{8}$ in. (22.2 × 27.6 cm.)
LITERATURE: Langdale, no. 89

The view is taken from the artist's top floor studio at 29 rue Terre Neuve, Meudon, looking up the street in the direction of the observatory terrace.

28. *Girl with Cat*. Before autumn 1921, probably late 1910s to early 1920s. (p. 27*)
New York, Metropolitan Museum of Art
Oil on canvas, $13\frac{3}{4} \times 10\frac{1}{2}$ in. (34.9 × 26.7 cm.). Signed and inscribed on the back, in pencil: *John/Enfant et Chat*
PROVENANCE: the artist, until *c.* March 1922; Jeanne Robert Foster, 1922–62; Maynard Walker Gallery, New York; Joan Whitney Payson, 1962; bequeathed by her to Metropolitan Museum of Art, 1975
EXHIBITED: Société du Salon d'Automne, Paris, 1921, no. 1209
LITERATURE: Langdale, no. 69

This is one of only two known signed paintings; the other is the early *Self-Portrait in a Red Blouse* (Cat. 4).

The sitter is the artist's most often used model (see Cat. 29–43); she first posed several years earlier for *Girl in a Blue Dress* (Cat. 16). The setting is Gwen John's studio at 29 rue Terre Neuve in Meudon.

Despite Gwen John's famous devotion to cats, they appear only infrequently in her paintings. The animal here is probably also the subject of *Black Cat on Blue and Pink* (Cat. 104). The drawing *Girl Holding a Cat* (Cat. 105) is closely related to this painting.

29. *Young Woman Holding a Black Cat*. Probably late 1910s to early 1920s. (p. 73)
London, The Trustees of the Tate Gallery
Oil on canvas, $18 \times 11\frac{5}{8}$ in. (45.7 × 29.5 cm.)
PROVENANCE: estate of the artist (P.J.27), until 1946; via Matthiesen, to the Tate Gallery
LITERATURE: Langdale, no. 72

See note to Cat. 28 (*Girl with Cat*).

30. *Girl Holding a Cat*. Probably late 1910s to early 1920s. (p. 73)
Upperville, Virginia, Paul Mellon Collection
Oil on canvas, $13\frac{1}{4} \times 10\frac{1}{4}$ in. (33.6 × 26 cm.) (sight)
PROVENANCE: estate of the artist (P.J.83), until 1964; via Faerber and Maison, to Maynard Walker Gallery, New York, 1964–5
LITERATURE: Langdale, no. 68

See note to Cat. 28 (*Girl with Cat*).

Traces of pencil drawing are clearly visible in this unfinished painting, particularly in the head of the cat.

31. *Girl Holding a Book*. Probably late 1910s to early 1920s. (p. 26*)
Northampton, Mass., Smith College Museum of Art
Oil on canvas, $17\frac{1}{2} \times 13\frac{1}{2}$ in. (44.4 × 34.3 cm.)
PROVENANCE: the artist, until 1930; via Carnegie Institute, to Rowland Burdon-Muller; anonymous gift to Smith College Museum of Art, 1972
EXHIBITED: Carnegie Institute, Pittsburgh, *29th Annual Exhibition*, 1930, no. 130
LITERATURE: Langdale, no. 73

See note to Cat. 28 (*Girl with Cat*).

32. *Study of a Young Girl*. Probably late 1910s to early 1920s. (p. 73)
Dublin, The Hugh Lane Municipal Gallery of Modern Art
Oil on canvas, $17\frac{1}{2} \times 14\frac{1}{2}$ in. (44.4 × 36.8 cm.)
PROVENANCE: A. E. Anderson, as of 1929; given by him to The Hugh Lane Municipal Gallery of Modern Art, 1929
EXHIBITED: ? Chenil, 1926, perhaps as no. 31 or 41
LITERATURE: Langdale, no. 74

See note to Cat. 28 (*Girl with Cat*).

33. *Seated Girl with Sewing*. Probably late 1910s to early 1920s. (p. 74)
Collection of Mrs R. Pilkington
Oil on canvas, $17\frac{3}{4} \times 14\frac{3}{4}$ in. (45.1 × 37.5 cm.)
PROVENANCE: estate of the artist (P.J.75), until 1961; via Matthiesen, to Mrs Geoffrey Colman
LITERATURE: Langdale, no. 78

See note to Cat. 28 (*Girl with Cat*).

34. *Girl in Blue*. *c.*1921. (p. 75)
Private collection
Oil on canvas, $18\frac{1}{4} \times 15$ in. (46.4 × 38.1 cm.)
PROVENANCE: the artist, until 1922; John Quinn, April 1922 until 1924; Julia Quinn Anderson (sister of John Quinn), until 1934; Mary Anderson (Mrs Thomas F.) Conroy (her daughter), until 1970
EXHIBITED: The Harvard

Society for Contemporary Art, Cambridge, Mass.

LITERATURE: John Quinn account book, p. 57; Langdale, no. 80

See note to Cat. 28 (*Girl with Cat*).

35. *Girl Holding a Rose.* Probably late 1910s to early 1920s. (p. 34*)

Upperville, Virginia, Paul Mellon Collection

Oil on canvas, $17\frac{3}{4} \times 14\frac{1}{2}$ in. (45.1 × 36.8 cm.)

PROVENANCE: estate of the artist (P.J.25), until 1959; via Matthiesen, to Crane Kalman Gallery, London; Mr and Mrs Sidney Gilliat, 1959–74; Christie's, London, 10 and 11 October 1974, lot 281, illus.; Davis & Long, 1974

LITERATURE: Langdale, no. 81

See note to Cat. 28 (*Girl with Cat*).

On the verso is a rather completely sketched variant of *Girl in Profile* (Cat. 25).

36. *Portrait of a Young Woman Wearing a Locket.* Probably late 1910s to early 1920s. (p. 75)

Collection of Ben John

Oil on canvas mounted on plywood, $13\frac{7}{8} \times 10\frac{7}{8}$ in. (35.2 × 27.6 cm.)

PROVENANCE: estate of the artist (P.J.65)

LITERATURE: Langdale, no. 86

See note to Cat. 28 (*Girl with Cat*).

37. *Seated Woman Wearing a Blue Bow.* Probably late 1910s to early 1920s. (p. 74)

Private collection

Oil on canvas, $16\frac{1}{4} \times 13$ in. (41.3 × 33 cm.)

PROVENANCE: estate of the artist (P.J.40), until 1962; via Matthiesen, to James Coats, until 1965; Davis, 1965

LITERATURE: Langdale, no. 93

See note to Cat. 28 (*Girl with Cat*).

38. *Girl in a Green Dress.* Probably late 1910s to early 1920s. (p. 74)

Cardiff, National Museum of Wales

Oil on canvas, $23\frac{1}{2} \times 15\frac{1}{2}$ in. (59.7 × 39.3 cm.)

PROVENANCE: estate of the artist (P.J.45); gift of Mr Edwin John (nephew of the artist) to the National Museum of Wales, 1970

LITERATURE: Langdale, no. 97

See note to Cat. 28 (*Girl with Cat*).

Although this sitter appears repeatedly, in rather similar poses, this is the only known example of precisely this composition; the overall greenish cast of the palette is also atypical.

39. *Young Woman Wearing a Large Hat.* Probably late 1910s to early 1920s. (p. 77)

Upperville, Virginia, Paul Mellon Collection

Oil on canvas, $18\frac{7}{8} \times 14\frac{3}{4}$ in. (47.9 × 37.5 cm.)

PROVENANCE: estate of the artist (P.J.13), until 1961; via Matthiesen to present owner 1961

LITERATURE: Langdale, no. 99

See note to Cat. 28 (*Girl with Cat*).

40. *Young Woman in a Red Shawl.* Probably late 1910s to early 1920s. (p. 75)

Private collection

Oil on canvas, $17\frac{1}{2} \times 13\frac{1}{2}$ in. (44.4 × 34.3 cm.)

PROVENANCE: estate of the artist (P.J.33), until 1946; via Matthiesen, to Edward Le Bas, until 1966

LITERATURE: Langdale, no. 101

See note to Cat. 28 (*Girl with Cat*).

41. *Woman with Cloak.* Probably late 1910s to early 1920s. (p. 74)

Buffalo, Albright-Knox Art Gallery

Oil on canvas, $25\frac{1}{4} \times 19\frac{1}{2}$ in. (64.1 × 49.5 cm.)

PROVENANCE: the artist; John Quinn, as of 1924; John Quinn estate, until 1926

EXHIBITED: Art Gallery of Ontario, Toronto, *Loan Exhibition of Portraits*, 1927, no. 53

LITERATURE: *John Quinn Collection*, p. 18; Langdale, no. 108

This is one of four very similar versions of this composition.

42. *The Convalescent.* Probably late 1910s to mid 1920s. (p. 35*)

Private collection

Oil on canvas, $15\frac{3}{4} \times 12\frac{3}{4}$ in. (40 × 32.4 cm.)

PROVENANCE: estate of the artist (P.J.16), until 1946; via Matthiesen, to Mr Hugo Pitman, London; Mrs Hugo Pitman, London; by descent to present owner

LITERATURE: Langdale, no. 116

This picture belongs to the largest known series in Gwen John's *oeuvre* (see Cat. 43), from which her most frequently used model derives her name.

43. *The Letter.* Probably late 1910s to mid 1920s, perhaps 1924. (p. 76)

Manchester City Art Galleries

Oil on canvas, $16\frac{1}{2} \times 13$ in. (41.9 × 33 cm.)

PROVENANCE: the artist; Charles L. Rutherston, 1924; donated by him to City of Manchester Art Gallery, 1925

EXHIBITED: Salon des Tuileries, Paris, 1924, no. 787; City Art Gallery and Museum, Cartwright Hall, Bradford, *Coming of Age*, 1925, no. 134

LITERATURE: Langdale, no. 111

See note to Cat. 42 (*The Convalescent*).

According to Charles L. Rutherston, this picture was painted in 1924; at least one version was begun as early as 1919.

44. *Interior (Rue Terre Neuve).* Probably early to mid 1920s. (p. 14*)

Manchester City Art Galleries

Oil on canvas, $8\frac{3}{4} \times 10\frac{5}{8}$ in. (22.2 × 27 cm.)

PROVENANCE: the artist, until 1924; Charles L. Rutherston, 1924; donated by him to City of Manchester Art Gallery, 1925

EXHIBITED: Salon des Tuileries, Paris, 1924, no. 788

LITERATURE: Langdale, no. 121

The painting's stretcher is inscribed by Charles Rutherston: *P 248 Interior (Meudon, near Paris) / by Gwen John.*

The setting of *Interior (Rue Terre Neuve)* is the artist's rue Terre Neuve studio, the same room which appears in so many portraits of the convalescent model (for example, Cat. 28, *Girl with Cat*).

45. *The Japanese Doll.* Probably early to late 1920s. (p. 18*)

Collection of Ben John

Oil on canvas, 12 × 16 in. (30.5 × 40.7 cm.)

PROVENANCE: estate of the artist (P.J.73)

LITERATURE: Langdale, no. 125

See note to Cat. 44 (*Interior (Rue Terre Neuve)*).

Another now complete version of the composition (private collection) is known to have been unfinished as late as 1928.

46. *Seated Nude.* c.1923–4. (p. 76)

Private collection

Oil on canvas, $17\frac{1}{2} \times 13\frac{1}{2}$ in. (44.4 × 34.3 cm.)

PROVENANCE: the artist, until *c.* March 1924; John Quinn, 1924; John Quinn estate, until 1927; American Art Galleries, 1927, lot 324; Julia Quinn Anderson (sister of John Quinn), until 1934; Mary Anderson (Mrs Thomas F.) Conroy (her daughter), until 1970

LITERATURE: ? *John Quinn Collection*, p. 18; Langdale, no. 126

Gwen John is known to have been working on this picture in 1923 and John Quinn received it early the following year. The unidentified model also posed for *Woman with Hands Crossed* (Cat. 47).

47. *Woman with Hands Crossed.* Probably *c.*1923–4. (p. 47*)

Collection of Carter Burden

Oil on canvas, $16\frac{1}{8} \times 13\frac{1}{8}$ in. (41 × 33.2 cm)

PROVENANCE: the artist; John Quinn, until 1924; John Quinn estate, until 1927; American Art Galleries, 1927, lot 468; Samuel Lustgarten, Chicago, and Sherman Oaks, California; Schweitzer Gallery, New York, until *c.*1966; private collection, until 1979; d'Offay

LITERATURE: *John Quinn Collection*, p. 18; Langdale, no. 129

See note to Cat. 46 (*Seated Nude*).

On the verso is an unfinished oil study of a different sitter.

48. *Girl with a Blue Scarf*. Probably c.1923–4. (p. 46*)

New York, The Museum of Modern Art

Oil on canvas, $16\frac{1}{4} \times 13$ in. (41.3 × 33 cm.)

PROVENANCE: the artist; John Quinn, until 1924; John Quinn estate, until 1927; American Art Galleries, 1927, lot 76; Miss Edith Wetmore, Newport, Rhode Island; Mr Nelson A. Sears, as of 1963; given by Nelson A. Sears in memory of Mrs Millicent A. Rogers to the Museum of Modern Art, 1963

LITERATURE: *John Quinn Collection*, p. 18; Langdale, no. 131

The setting of *Girl with a Blue Scarf* is the artist's studio at 29 rue Terre Neuve in Meudon. The unidentified model posed for a series of paintings wearing a mulberry-coloured dress.

49. *Still Life with a Vase of Flowers and an Inkwell*. Probably late 1920s. (p. 78)

Private collection

Oil on canvas, $10\frac{1}{2} \times 8\frac{1}{2}$ in. (26.6 × 21.6 cm.)

PROVENANCE: estate of the artist (P.J.87), until 1970; via Faerber and Maison, to private collection

LITERATURE: Langdale, no. 141

This is one of several late still-life paintings which contain new objects: the prayer book, boldly patterned shawl, and inkwell have not appeared before. The white vase, holding a similar arrangement of leaves and flowers, is the subject of various watercolours of the time (see Cat. 110).

50. *Portrait of Miss Bridget Sarah Bishop*. 1929. (p. 77)

Estate of the artist (P.J.46)

Oil on canvas mounted on wood, $15\frac{3}{4} \times 12\frac{1}{4}$ in. (40 × 31.1 cm.) (sight)

LITERATURE: Langdale, no. 148

This portrait was commissioned by Bridget Sarah Bishop's mother Louise Salaman Bishop, a member of the Salaman family Gwen John had met at the Slade. The sitter, eighteen at the time and a student at the Sorbonne, posed twice a week at the rue Terre Neuve during the spring of 1929. For several years thereafter, Mrs Bishop inquired repeatedly about the painting, to no avail; the artist apparently considered it unfinished and kept it in her studio.

51. *Girl Praying*. Probably c.1930. (p. 15*)

Collection of Mr and Mrs D. Little

Oil on canvas, 17 × 11 in. (43.2 × 27.9 cm.)

PROVENANCE: estate of the artist (P.J.38), until 1982; via d'Offay, to private collection

LITERATURE: Langdale, no. 151

The child is unidentified. Amongst the artist's papers are sketches dated 1930 of this composition.

52. *Girl by a Window*. Probably c.1931. (p. 42)

Collection of E. Pace Barnes

Oil and pencil on paper, $7\frac{1}{4} \times 5\frac{1}{4}$ in. (18.4 × 13.3 cm.). Stamped at lower right: Gwen John (estate stamp)

PROVENANCE: estate of the artist (E.J.334), until 1958; via Matthiesen, to the Marchioness of Cholmondeley, 1958–73; Sotheby's, London, 12–13 July 1973, illus.; Davis, 1973; private collection, New York, until 1975; Davis & Long

LITERATURE: Langdale, no. 155

Amongst the artist's papers is a sheet of related sketches dated 1931, a date probably approximately correct for this painting as well, making it one of Gwen John's last works in oil. It is closer in conception to the late gouaches (for example, Cat. 120) than to other late paintings; indeed, other versions of this composition (National Museum of Wales, Cardiff) are executed in a mixture of oil and gouache.

53. *Winifred John in a Large Hat*. Probably c.1895–8. (p. 48)

Cardiff, National Museum of Wales

Charcoal on paper, $12\frac{1}{4} \times 9\frac{1}{2}$ in. (31.1 × 24.1 cm.)

PROVENANCE: the artist; Augustus John, until 1961; Dorothy (Dorelia) McNeill (Mrs Augustus John), until 1969; private collection; Anthony Reed, London, as of 1975

LITERATURE: Langdale, no. 156

See Cat. 1 for a painting of Winifred John. Gwen John's younger sister was the model for a number of the artist's early drawings (see Cat. 54–6).

54. *A Woman Asleep on a Sofa*. Probably c.1895–8. (p. 48)

Private collection

Pencil and wash on paper, $6\frac{1}{8} \times 7\frac{7}{8}$ in. (15.6 × 19.6 cm.). Stamped at lower right: Gwen John (estate stamp)

PROVENANCE: estate of the artist (E.J.205), until 1966; via Faerber and Maison, to Davis

LITERATURE: Langdale, no. 161

See note to Cat. 53 (*Winifred John in a Large Hat*).

55. *Portrait of Winifred John*. Probably c.1895–8. (p. 48)

Sheffield City Art Galleries

Pencil on tan paper, $6\frac{1}{4} \times 6\frac{1}{4}$ in. (15.9 × 15.9 cm.). Stamped at lower left: Gwen John (estate stamp)

PROVENANCE: estate of the artist (E.J.58); via Matthiesen, to M. Georges Wildenstein; Thos. Agnew & Sons, London, 1964

LITERATURE: Langdale, no. 160

See note to Cat. 53 (*Winifred John in a Large Hat*).

56. *Seated Girl with Hat (Winifred John)*. Probably c.1895–8. (p. 48)

Private collection

Charcoal on paper, $12\frac{5}{8} \times 9\frac{1}{2}$ in. (32 × 24.1 cm.)

PROVENANCE: estate of the artist (E.J.491), until 1982; via d'Offay, to present owner

See note to Cat. 53 (*Winifred John in a Large Hat*).

57. *Portrait Group*. Probably c.1897–8. (p. 49)

Private collection

Watercolour and pencil on paper, 11 × 15 in. (27.9 × 38.1 cm.)

PROVENANCE: the artist; Lady Clarke Hall, until 1950; Mrs F. W. Samuel, 1950–2; by descent to present owner

LITERATURE: Langdale, no. 165

See note to Cat. 1 (*Portrait of the Artist's Sister Winifred*).

Rosa Waugh stands at left, Winifred John and Michel Salaman sit at a table, and Augustus John slouches behind them; through the window a strolling couple is seen: the woman is said to be Gwen John herself. *Portrait Group* was almost certainly done in 1897–8, in London, when Winifred John was living there with her sister and brother.

The first and second owners of the picture were Slade contemporaries of the Johns, Lady Clarke Hall (as Edna Waugh), and Mrs F. W. Samuel (as Dorothy Salaman).

58. *Portrait of Dorelia at Toulouse*. 1903–4. (p. 52)

London, The Trustees of the British Museum

Red chalk on paper, $12\frac{7}{8} \times 9\frac{7}{8}$ in. (32.7 × 25.1 cm.)

PROVENANCE: estate of the artist (E.J.443), until 1982; via d'Offay, to British Museum, 1982

LITERATURE: Langdale, no. 167

See note to Cat. 6 (*The Student*).

Although this sheet is not specifically a study for *The Student* (Cat. 6), Dorelia is attired identically; like the painting, the drawing was executed in Toulouse during the winter of 1903–4.

59. *The Cat*. Probably c.1905–8. (p. 38*)

London, The Trustees of the Tate Gallery

Watercolour and pencil on paper, $4\frac{3}{8} \times 5\frac{3}{8}$ in. (11.1 × 13.7 cm.)

PROVENANCE: estate of the artist, until 1940; via Matthiesen, to the Tate Gallery

LITERATURE: Langdale, no. 173

This white-fronted tortoise-shell cat is the subject of most of Gwen John's early drawings of cats (see Cat. 60–2); she also appears in *La Chambre sur la Cour* (Cat. 9). She disappeared in 1908, to the artist's extreme distress.

60. *Study of a Tortoise-shell Cat.* Probably *c.*1905–8. (p. 60)
Private collection
Watercolour and pencil on paper, 6¼ × 4⅞ in. (15.9 × 12.4 cm.) Stamped at lower right: Gwen John (estate stamp)
PROVENANCE: estate of the artist (E.J.870), until 1977; via d'Offay, to Davis & Long
See note to Cat. 59 (*The Cat*).

61. *Sketch of a Seated Cat.* Probably *c.* 1905–8. (p. 60)
London, Victoria and Albert Museum
Watercolour and pencil, 6⅛ × 4⅝ in. (15.5 × 11.7 cm.). Stamped at lower right: Gwen John (estate stamp)
PROVENANCE: estate of the artist (probably E.J.196), until 1946; via Matthiesen, to Victoria and Albert Museum
LITERATURE: Langdale, no. 178
See note to Cat. 59 (*The Cat*).

62. *Cat.* Probably *c.*1905–8
London, The Trustees of the Tate Gallery. (p. 60).
Watercolour and Chinese white on paper, 4¾ × 6¼ in. (12.1 × 15.9 cm.)
PROVENANCE: gift of the artist to Miss Mary Constance Lloyd; given by her to the Tate Gallery, 1957
LITERATURE: Langdale, no. 175
See note to Cat. 59 (*The Cat*).
Mary Constance Lloyd, the first owner of the picture, was an artist friend of Gwen John in Paris; Gwen posed for her in 1906 and 1907.

63. *Woman Dressing.* Probably *c.*1907. (p. 53)
Collection of Howard Kopet
Wash and Chinese white on paper, 10¾ × 9 in. (27.3 × 22.9 cm.) Stamped at lower right: Gwen John (estate stamp)
PROVENANCE: estate of the artist (E.J.555), until 1974; via Stefanie Maison, to Davis & Long
LITERATURE: Langdale, no. 180
The model and the room are unidentified. The latter may well be the Paris interior that is the setting for *La Chambre sur la Cour* (Cat. 9), and probably for *Girl Reading at the Window* (Cat. 15).

64. *Female Nude Standing, Right Hand on Hip.* Perhaps *c.*1907–9. (p. 52)
Cardiff, National Museum of Wales
Pencil on brown paper, 9 × 6¼ in. (22.9 × 15.8 cm.)
PROVENANCE: estate of the artist, until 1976

65. *Self-Portrait.* Probably *c.*1907–9. (p. 8)
Private collection
Pencil and wash on tan paper, 10 × 8¼ in. (25.4 × 20.9 cm.)
PROVENANCE: private collection, from at least 1946; thence to present owner
LITERATURE: Langdale, no. 182
This drawing has often been exhibited as *Self-Portrait at the Age of about Twenty Years.* In fact, it dates to at least a decade later, to about 1907–9, having been executed at much the same time as *The Artist in her Room in Paris* (Cat. 11).

66. *Self-Portrait, Naked, Sitting on a Bed.* Probably 1909. (p. 52)
Private collection
Pencil and gouache on paper, 10 × 6⅜ in. (25.4 × 16.2 cm.)
PROVENANCE: estate of the artist (E.J.942), until 1982; via d'Offay, to present owner
LITERATURE: Langdale, no. 183
See note to Cat. 11 (*The Artist in her Room in Paris*).
The setting is Gwen John's room at 87 rue du Cherche-Midi. In a 1909 letter to her friend Ursula Tyrwhitt, the artist described drawing a series of self-portraits in an interior; this is probably one of that series.

67. *Self-Portrait Holding a Letter.* Probably *c.*1907–9. (p. 53)
Paris, Musée Rodin
Watercolour and pencil on paper, 8¾ × 6⅜ in. (22.3 × 16.1 cm.)
PROVENANCE: the artist; gift to Auguste Rodin
See note to Cat. 65 (*Self-Portrait*).

68. *Head of a Young Woman.* Probably *c.*1909. (p. 56)
Yale University Art Gallery
Pencil and wash on paper, 10⅞ × 7¾ in. (27.6 × 19.7 cm.) (sight). Stamped at lower left: Gwen John (estate stamp)
PROVENANCE: estate of the artist (E.J.48), until 1952; via Matthiesen, to Maynard Walker Gallery, New York; Mr and Mrs James Fosburgh; bequeathed by them to Yale University Art Gallery, 1978
LITERATURE: Langdale, no. 184
The sitter is unidentified.

69. *Portrait of a Lady, Half-Length, Leaning Back.* *c.*1910. (p. 56)
Collection of Terry Davis
Pencil and wash on paper, 10 × 6¾ in. (25.4 × 17.1 cm.). Stamped at lower left: Gwen John (estate stamp)
PROVENANCE: estate of the artist (E.J.35), until 1946; via Matthiesen, to Mrs J. Cheever Cowdin, until *c.*1963; Davis
LITERATURE: Langdale, no. 192
This unidentified model, known as 'a lady', is the subject of a series of drawings (see Cat. 70 and 71) and an etching (Cat. 72). These pictures have erroneously sometimes been called self-portraits.

70. *Portrait of a Lady.* *c.*1910. (p. 56)
Borough of Thamesdown Museums and Art Gallery
Pencil and wash on paper, 9⅝ × 6¼ in. (24.5 × 16 cm.). Stamped at lower left: Gwen John (estate stamp)
PROVENANCE: estate of the artist (E.J.266), until 1947; via Matthiesen, to Swindon (Borough of Thamesdown) Museums and Art Gallery
LITERATURE: Langdale, no. 194
See note to Cat. 69 (*Portrait of a Lady, Half-Length, Leaning Back*).

71. *Portrait of a Lady.* *c.*1910. (p. 56)
London, private collection
Pencil and wash on tan paper, 9½ × 6⅛ in. (24 × 15.7 cm.). Stamped at lower right: Gwen John (estate stamp)
PROVENANCE: estate of the artist (E.J.173), until 1946; via Matthiesen, to present owner
LITERATURE: Langdale, no. 193
See note to Cat. 69 (*Portrait of a Lady, Half-Length, Leaning Back*).

72. *Head of a Lady.* *c.*1910. (p. 56)
Private collection
Etching on paper, 5 × 3½ in. (12.7 × 8.9 cm.)
PROVENANCE: estate of the artist (E.J.213), until at least 1946; private collection, until *c.*1978; Michael Parkin Fine Art Ltd., London
LITERATURE: Langdale, no. 197
See note to Cat. 69 (*Portrait of a Lady, Half-Length, Leaning Back*).
In a letter probably written in 1910 to Ursula Tyrwhitt, the artist discussed making two etchings, one of which was certainly this picture.

73. *Étude pour 'Les Suppliantes'.* *c.*1910. (p. 61)
Private collection
Pencil and wash on tan paper, 9⅝ × 7⅞ in. (24.3 × 20 cm.) (sight)
PROVENANCE: the artist, until 1914; John Quinn, until 1924; John Quinn estate, until 1926; A. Conger Goodyear, Buffalo and New York; given by him to Anna Dunbar; Parke-Bernet Galleries, New York, sale 2635, 13 December 1967, lot 25
LITERATURE: John Quinn ledger, pp. 117, 176; *John Quinn Collection*, p. 18, illus. p. 148; Langdale, no. 188
See note to Cat. 8 (*Chloe Boughton-Leigh*).
*Étude pour 'Les Suppliantes'* is probably the artist's title; however, there is no known painting called *Les Suppliantes*, nor is there one for which such a name would seem appropriate.
The sheet is one of a group of drawings of Chloe Boughton-Leigh (see Cat. 74) of about

1910, all of which relate closely to the second painting of the subject (Cat. 14). They were once thought to be portraits of Fenella Lovell (see Cat. 12 and 13).

This and *Bust of a Woman* (Cat. 74) were the first two drawings Gwen John sold to John Quinn; she sent them to him in 1914 along with the related painting, *Chloe Boughton-Leigh* (Cat. 14).

74. *Bust of a Woman*. *c.*1910. (p. 61)

Buffalo, Albright-Knox Art Gallery

Pencil and wash on paper, $9\frac{5}{8} \times 7\frac{1}{2}$ in. (24.4 × 19 cm.)

PROVENANCE: the artist, until 1914; John Quinn, until 1924; John Quinn estate, until 1927; American Art Galleries, 1927, lot 36; A. Conger Goodyear, Buffalo and New York; given by him to Albright-Knox Art Gallery, 1953

LITERATURE: John Quinn ledger, pp. 117, 176; *John Quinn Collection*, p. 18; Langdale, no. 190

See note to Cat. 73 (*Étude pour 'Les Suppliantes'*).

75. *Woman and Child in a Railway Carriage*. Probably 1910s. (p. 64)

Private collection

Gouache, watercolour, and pencil on paper, $7\frac{3}{4} \times 6$ in. (19.7 × 15.2 cm). Stamped at lower right: Gwen John (estate stamp)

PROVENANCE: estate of the artist (E.J.62), until 1946; via Matthiesen, to Mrs Heygate, London; Mr and Mrs Ronald Tree, New York, until 1976; Sotheby Parke-Bernet, Inc., New York, 8 and 9 October 1976, lot 216, illus.; Davis & Long, until 1977

The subject is one to which the artist returned at the end of her career (see Cat. 123).

76. *Profile of a Bourgeois Couple*. Probably 1910s. (p. 64)

Collection of Howard Kopet

Gouache, watercolour, and pencil on paper, $8 \times 6\frac{1}{4}$ in. (20.3 × 15.9 cm.). Stamped at lower right: Gwen John (estate stamp)

PROVENANCE: estate of the artist (E.J.271), until 1946; via Matthiesen, to Mrs J. Cheever Cowdin, until 1964; Davis

LITERATURE: Langdale, no. 199

77. *Back View of a Soldier, Standing, in Conversation with a Girl*. *c.*1914–18. (p. 65)

Collection of Carter Burden

Watercolour and pencil on paper, $8\frac{1}{4} \times 6\frac{1}{2}$ in. (20.9 × 16.5 cm.) (sight). Stamped at lower left: Gwen John (estate stamp)

PROVENANCE: estate of the artist (E.J.51), until 1946; via Matthiesen, to Mrs J. Cheever Cowdin, New York, until 1969; Davis, 1969

LITERATURE: Langdale, no. 229

This is one of the very few pictures by Gwen John in which she makes direct reference to World War I.

78. *Seated Nun and Standing Woman in Church*. Probably 1910s. (p. 64)

Private collection

Gouache, watercolour, and pencil on paper, $6\frac{1}{4} \times 4\frac{7}{8}$ in. (16 × 12.4 cm.)

PROVENANCE: the artist; gift to Véra Oumançoff, until 1959; Jacques and Raïssa Maritain (her sister and brother-in-law); private collection, until 1977; Davis & Long

LITERATURE: Langdale, no. 207

This is one of many views in Meudon church made by the artist during the 1910s and 1920s. The figures, generally female, are usually seen from the rear. The nun belongs to the Meudon chapter of the Soeurs de Charité Dominicaines de la Présentation de la Sainte Vierge de Tours.

79. *Young Woman in a Hat*. Probably 1910s. (p. 64)

Stanford University Museum of Art

Watercolour, gouache and pencil on paper, $6\frac{1}{2} \times 5$ in. (16.5 × 12.7 cm.)

PROVENANCE: the artist; John Quinn, as of 1924; John Quinn estate, until 1927; American Art Galleries, 1927, lot 385; Julia Quinn Anderson (sister of John Quinn), until 1934; Mary Anderson (Mrs Thomas F.) Conroy (her daughter) until 1970; Thomas F. Conroy (her husband); Thomas A. Conroy (his son); given by him to Stanford University Museum of Art, 1976

See note to Cat. 78 (*Seated Nun and Standing Woman in Church*).

80. *Little Fair-Haired Boy Standing in Church*. Probably 1910s. (p. 65)

Collection of Carter Burden

Watercolour and pencil on paper, $8\frac{1}{2} \times 6\frac{1}{4}$ in. (21.6 × 15.9 cm.)

PROVENANCE: the artist; gift to Véra Oumançoff, until 1959; Jacques and Raïssa Maritain (her sister and brother-in-law); private collection, until 1968; Sotheby's, London, 11 December 1968, lot 245; Thos. Agnew & Sons, London, 1968–9; Davis, 1969

LITERATURE: Langdale, no. 204

See note to Cat. 78 (*Seated Nun and Standing Woman in Church*).

81. *Girl Praying, Back View*. Probably 1910s. (p. 65)

Stanford University Museum of Art

Watercolour, gouache, and pencil on paper, $6\frac{1}{2} \times 5$in. (16.5 × 12.7 cm.)

PROVENANCE: as for Cat. 79

See note to Cat. 78 (*Seated Nun and Standing Woman in Church*).

82. *Two Women in Church*. Probably 1910s. (p. 66)

Collection of Mrs Martha Hare

Watercolour and pencil on paper, $10\frac{1}{4} \times 7\frac{7}{8}$ in. (25.9 × 20 cm.). Stamped at lower right: Gwen John (estate stamp)

PROVENANCE: estate of the artist (E.J.572), until 1978; via d'Offay, to Davis & Long

See note to Cat. 78 (*Seated Nun and Standing Woman in Church*).

83. *Seated Girl*. Probably 1910s. (p. 66)

Private collection

Watercolour and pencil on paper, $6\frac{1}{2} \times 4\frac{7}{8}$ in. (16.5 × 12.4 cm.)

PROVENANCE: as for Cat. 79, until 1970; private collection, 1970

See note to Cat. 78 (*Seated Nun and Standing Woman in Church*).

84. *A Nun and Two Girls in Church*. Probably 1910s. (p. 67)

Private collection

Watercolour and pencil on paper, $6\frac{3}{8} \times 5$ in. (16.2 × 12.7 cm.)

PROVENANCE: estate of the artist (E.J.674), until 1982; via d'Offay, to present owner

See note to Cat. 78 (*Seated Nun and Standing Woman in Church*).

The little girls in white-collared uniforms are orphans from the Orphelinat St. Joseph, run by the Meudon chapter of the Soeurs de Charité Dominicaines de la Présentation de la Sainte Vierge de Tours.

85. *A Girl and an Older Woman in Church*. Probably 1910s. (p. 67)

Private collection

Watercolour and pencil on paper, $7\frac{7}{8} \times 5\frac{1}{8}$ in. (20 × 13 cm.)

PROVENANCE: estate of the artist (E.J.739), until 1982; via d'Offay, to present owner

See note to Cat. 78 (*Seated Nun and Standing Woman in Church*).

86. *Seated Woman, Dressed in Black*. Probably 1910s. (p. 66)

Collection of Carter Burden

Watercolour, gouache, and pencil on paper, $7 \times 6\frac{1}{4}$ in. (17.8 × 15.8 cm.). Stamped at lower right: Gwen John (estate stamp)

PROVENANCE: the artist, until 6 August 1928; gift to Véra Oumançoff, until 1959; Jacques and Raïssa Maritain (her sister and brother-in-law); private collection, until 1968; Sotheby's, London, 11 December 1968, lot 241, illus.; Mr and Mrs John Stanley-Clarke, until 1973; Sotheby's, London, 14 March 1973, lot 29; Davis

LITERATURE: Langdale, no. 217

See note to Cat. 78 (*Seated Nun and Standing Woman in Church*).

The original mount, now lost, is said to have been inscribed with a dedication to

Véra Oumançoff: *Portrait. Aout 6. 28.* The picture never belonged to the artist's estate; the stamp was applied as a verification of authenticity.

87. *Young Girl in Hooded Cloak.* Probably 1910s. (p. 67)
Private collection
Watercolour and gouache on paper, $8\frac{7}{8} \times 6\frac{7}{8}$ in. (22.5 × 17.5 cm.)
PROVENANCE: as for Cat. 83
See note to Cat. 78 (*Seated Nun and Standing Woman in Church*).

88. *Mademoiselle Pouvereau.* Probably 1910s. (p. 65)
San Francisco, private collection
Watercolour, gouache, and pencil on paper, $6\frac{7}{8} \times 5\frac{3}{8}$ in. (17.5 × 13.7 cm.). Stamped at upper right: Gwen John (estate stamp)
PROVENANCE: estate of the artist (E.J.400), until 1964; via Faerber and Maison, to Rex Evans, 1964–8
LITERATURE: Langdale, no. 210

89. *Little Girl with a Large Hat and Straw-Coloured Hair.* Probably late 1910s. (p. 63*)
Private collection
Gouache, watercolour, and pencil on paper, $8\frac{1}{2} \times 6\frac{3}{4}$ in. (21.6 × 17.2 cm.)
PROVENANCE: the artist, until 29 May 1928; gift to Véra Oumançoff, until 1959; Jacques and Raïssa Maritain (her sister and brother-in-law); private collection, until 1975; Davis & Long, 1975
LITERATURE: Langdale, no. 291
See note to Cat. 23 (*La Petite Modèle*).
The original mount, now lost, is said to have been inscribed with a dedication to Véra Oumançoff: *Petite fille dans le train (vous.) Mai 29.28.* This is one of a series of closely related drawings.

90. *A Corner of the Artist's Room, Rue Terre Neuve.* Probably late 1910s. (p. 72)
Private collection
Watercolour, pencil, and gouache, $9\frac{3}{4} \times 8\frac{3}{4}$ in. (24.7 × 22.2 cm.)
PROVENANCE: estate of the artist (E.J.905), until 1982; via d'Offay, to present owner
This corner of the artist's Meudon studio frequently appears in paintings of the same time (for example, Cat. 31).

91. *Study of Young Boy with Hands Clasped.* Probably late 1910s.
Collection of Terry Davis
Charcoal and wash on paper, $12\frac{3}{4} \times 8\frac{3}{4}$ in. (32.4 × 22.2 cm.). Stamped at lower left: Gwen John (estate stamp)
PROVENANCE: estate of the artist (E.J.18), until 1958; via Matthiesen, to Philip Robinson; Faerber and Maison, as of *c.*1965
LITERATURE: Langdale, no. 262
This unidentified boy is probably one of the Breton peasant children who sat for Gwen John during her stays in Finistère and Pléneuf during the late teens; he is the subject of a number of drawings (see Cat. 92).

92. *Breton Boy.* Probably late 1910s. (p. 70)
Private collection
Wash on paper, $11\frac{1}{4} \times 11$ in. (28.7 × 28 cm.). Stamped at lower left: Gwen John (estate stamp)
PROVENANCE: estate of the artist (E.J.866); d'Offay; Davis & Langdale, as of 1981
LITERATURE: Langdale, no. 264
See note to Cat. 91 (*Study of Young Boy with Hands Clasped*).

93. *Seated Girl with Folded Arms.* Probably late 1910s. (p. 71)
Private collection
Wash on tan paper, $12\frac{1}{2} \times 9\frac{7}{8}$ in. (31.9 × 25.1 cm.)
PROVENANCE: the artist; gift to Véra Oumançoff, until 1959; Jacques and Raïssa Maritain (her sister and brother-in-law); private collection, until 1976
LITERATURE: Langdale, no. 246
See note to Cat. 91 (*Study of Young Boy with Hands Clasped*).
This girl sat for a number of drawings; she has sometimes been incorrectly identified as Rosamund Manson.

94. *Three-Quarter-Length of a Young Woman with High Cheekbones.* Probably late 1910s. (p. 70)
Bedford, The Trustees of the Cecil Higgins Art Gallery
Wash on paper, $11 \times 9\frac{1}{2}$ in. (27.9 × 24.1 cm.). Stamped at lower right: Gwen John (estate stamp)
PROVENANCE: estate of the artist (E.J.70); until 1958; via Matthiesen, to the Cecil Higgins Art Gallery, 1958
LITERATURE: Langdale, no. 261
See note to Cat. 91 (*Study of Young Boy with Hands Clasped*).

95. *The Child with a Polo.* Probably late 1910s. (p. 70)
Private collection
Charcoal pencil on paper, $9\frac{1}{8} \times 8\frac{3}{4}$ in. (23.3 × 22.2 cm.). Inscribed on the back of the mount: *the child with a polo*
PROVENANCE: the artist; gift to Isabel Bowser; Lucy Bowser Featherston (her sister); private collection, by descent, until 1978; Christie's, London, 17 November 1978, lot 51; Davis & Long, 1978–80
LITERATURE: Langdale, no. 251
See note to Cat. 91 (*Study of Young Boy with Hands Clasped*).
This unidentified child posed for a series of drawings. Isabel Bowser, the first owner, was a close friend of the artist.

96. *Elisabeth de Willman Grabowska.* Probably late 1910s. (p. 69)
London, Victoria and Albert Museum
Wash on tan paper, $11\frac{3}{4} \times 9\frac{7}{8}$ in. (29.9 × 25 cm.)
PROVENANCE: estate of the artist (E.J.20), until 1946; via Matthiesen, to Victoria and Albert Museum
LITERATURE: Langdale, no. 270
Elisabeth de Willman Grabowska is the subject of many drawings by Gwen John; she is sometimes known as 'the girl with a sulky expression'. She lived in Paris but summered in Pléneuf, where her portraits may have been done.

97. *A Rag Doll.* Probably late 1910s. (p. 68)
Private collection
Wash on paper, $8\frac{1}{8} \times 6\frac{3}{4}$ in. (20.6 × 17.2 cm.). Stamped at lower right: Gwen John (estate stamp)
PROVENANCE: estate of the artist (E.J.887), until 1982; via d'Offay, to present owner
LITERATURE: Langdale, no. 268
In a number of the drawings of Elisabeth de Willman Grabowska (see Cat. 96), she holds a doll like this one.

98. *Louise Gautier Wearing a Cape.* Probably 1918 or 1919. (p. 68)
Private collection
Charcoal and wash on paper, $12\frac{1}{8} \times 10\frac{7}{8}$ in. (30.9 × 27.6 cm.)
PROVENANCE: the artist; gift to Isabel Bowser; Lucy Bowser Featherston (her sister); by descent to present owner
EXHIBITED: ? Société du Salon d'Automne, Paris, 1919, no. 967
LITERATURE: Langdale, no. 281
Louise Gautier was one of the Pléneuf peasant children who posed for Gwen John during her stays there in 1918 and 1919. The drawing is reminiscent of the paintings of a cloaked woman (see Cat. 41) of much the same date.
Like Cat. 95, 101, and 102, the sheet belonged to the artist's close friend Isabel Bowser.

99. *Girl with Plaits and a High-Crowned Hat.* Probably 1918 or 1919. (p. 68)
Duke of Devonshire
Charcoal and wash on paper, $12\frac{1}{2} \times 9\frac{1}{2}$ in. (31.7 × 24.1 cm.). Stamped at lower left: Gwen John (estate stamp)
PROVENANCE: estate of the artist, until 1958; via Matthiesen, to the Duke of Devonshire (then the Marquis of Hartington), 1958
LITERATURE: Langdale, no. 282
See note to Cat. 98 (*Louise Gautier Wearing a Cape*).
The child is Odette Litalien, the daughter of a Pléneuf farmer; she posed for a number of drawings.

100. *Child Posing.* Probably 1918 or 1919. (p. 69)

Private collection

Charcoal on paper, $9\frac{3}{8} \times 8\frac{1}{4}$ in. (23.7 × 20.9 cm.). Inscribed on the back of the mount: *Child posing. March 26 28*

PROVENANCE: the artist, until 26 March 1928; gift to Véra Oumançoff, until 1959; Jacques and Raïssa Maritain (her sister and brother-in-law); private collection, until 1978

LITERATURE: Langdale, no. 288

The model is Marie Hamonet, one of the Pléneuf children who posed for Gwen John in 1918 and 1919; she is the subject of a number of drawings (see Cat. 101 and 102).

101. *Girl with Hands in her Lap.* Probably 1918 or 1919. (p. 69)

Cambridge, Fitzwilliam Museum

Charcoal and wash on paper, $12\frac{1}{2} \times 9\frac{3}{4}$ in. (31.7 × 24.8 cm.)

PROVENANCE: the artist; gift to Isabel Bowser; private collection, by descent, until 1981; d'Offay

LITERATURE: Langdale, no. 286

See note to Cat. 100 (*Child Posing*).

102. *Marie Hamonet with Arms Crossed.* Probably 1918 or 1919. (p. 68)

Private collection

Charcoal and wash on paper, $12\frac{5}{8} \times 9\frac{7}{8}$ in. (32 × 25 cm.)

PROVENANCE: as for Cat. 98

See note to Cat. 100 (*Child Posing*).

103. *Profile of Arthur Symons.* Probably 1921. (p. 71)

Collection of E. Pace Barnes

Charcoal on paper, $9\frac{3}{4} \times 8\frac{7}{8}$ in. (24.8 × 22.5 cm.) (sight). Stamped at lower right: Gwen John (estate stamp)

PROVENANCE: estate of the artist (E.J.231), until 1969; via Faerber and Maison, to Davis, 1969; private collection, 1969–75; Davis & Long

LITERATURE: Langdale, no. 301

The poet and critic Arthur Symons is the subject of a series of drawings by Gwen John. The artist met Symons and his wife Rhoda in 1920, and visited them the following summer at Island Cottage, their house at Wittersham, Kent; it was probably during that stay that she did the drawings.

104. *Black Cat on Blue and Pink.* Probably late 1910s to early 1920s. (p. 39*)

Collection of Ben John

Watercolour, gouache, and pencil on paper, $6\frac{3}{4} \times 8\frac{1}{2}$ in. (17.1 × 21.7 cm.)

PROVENANCE: estate of the artist

See note to Cat. 28 (*Girl with Cat*).

105. *Girl Holding a Cat.* Probably late 1910s to early 1920s. (p. 73)

Private collection

Pencil on paper, $9\frac{7}{8} \times 6\frac{3}{8}$ in. (25.1 × 16.2 cm.). Stamped at lower right: Gwen John (estate stamp)

PROVENANCE: estate of the artist (E.J.892), until 1981; via d'Offay, to Davis & Langdale

This drawing is closely related to the painting *Girl with Cat* (Cat. 28). The inscribed numbers are colour notations.

106. *At Meudon.* Probably late 1910s to early 1920s. (p. 78)

University of Manchester, Whitworth Art Gallery

Watercolour, gouache, pencil, and black chalk on paper, $6\frac{5}{8} \times 7\frac{7}{8}$ in. (16.8 × 20 cm.)

PROVENANCE: Dr E. J. Sidebotham, 1926; presented by him to the Whitworth Art Gallery

EXHIBITED: ? Chenil, 1926

See Cat. 27, *Rue Terre Neuve, Meudon*, for a similar view.

107. *Study of Marigolds.* Probably late 1910s to early 1920s. (p. 30*)

Private collection

Watercolour and pencil on paper, $6\frac{7}{8} \times 8\frac{7}{8}$ in. (17.5 × 22.5 cm.). Stamped at lower left: Gwen John (estate stamp)

PROVENANCE: estate of the artist (E.J.577), until 1976; via d'Offay, to present owner

There are extensive colour notes in the right margin.

108. *A Vase of Flowers, with Colour Notes.* Probably 1920s. (p. 79)

Cardiff, National Museum of Wales

Watercolour and pencil on paper, $6\frac{1}{4} \times 5$ in. (15.9 × 12.7 cm.)

PROVENANCE: estate of the artist, until 1976

109. *Flowers and Brown Bowl.* Probably 1920s. (p. 79)

Collection of Carter Burden

Gouache and pencil on paper, $9\frac{1}{8} \times 8\frac{1}{2}$ in. (23.2 × 21.6 cm.). Stamped at lower right: Gwen John (estate stamp)

PROVENANCE: estate of the artist (E.J.704), until 1981; via d'Offay, to Davis & Langdale

110. *Ivy Leaves in a White Jug.* Probably 1920s. (p. 79)

Cardiff, National Museum of Wales

Gouache and pencil on paper, $6\frac{1}{2} \times 5$ in. (16.5 × 12.7 cm.)

PROVENANCE: estate of the artist, until 1976

See note to Cat. 49 (*Still Life with a Vase of Flowers and an Inkwell*).

111. *Study for Girl in a Mulberry-Coloured Dress.* c.1923–4.

Cardiff, National Museum of Wales

Black chalk on brown paper, $8\frac{1}{2} \times 6\frac{1}{2}$ in. (21.6 × 16.5 cm.)

PROVENANCE: estate of the artist, until 1976

See note to Cat. 48 (*Girl with a Blue Scarf*).

112. *Two Girls in Church.* Probably 1920s. (p. 81)

Collection of Mrs Martha Hare

Watercolour, gouache, and black chalk on paper, $8\frac{3}{4} \times 6\frac{7}{8}$ in. (22.1 × 17.4 cm.)

PROVENANCE: the artist; gift to Véra Oumançoff, until 1959; Jacques and Raïssa Maritain (her sister and brother-in-law); private collection, until 1975; Sotheby's, London, 25 June 1975, lot 33; Davis & Long

LITERATURE: Langdale, no. 312

See note to Cat. 78 (*Seated Nun and Standing Woman in Church*).

Another version of this composition (private collection) belonged to John Quinn; that picture and probably this one predate the collector's death in 1924.

113. *Two Girls Kneeling in Church.* Probably 1920s. (p. 80)

Private collection

Gouache and watercolour on paper, $4\frac{7}{8} \times 3\frac{3}{8}$ in (12.4 × 8.6 cm.). Stamped at lower right: Gwen John (estate stamp)

PROVENANCE: estate of the artist (E.J.646), until 1977; via d'Offay, to Davis & Long; private collection; thence to present owner

LITERATURE: Langdale, no. 311

See note to Cat. 78 (*Seated Nun and Standing Woman in Church*).

114. *Woman and Two Nuns in Church.* Probably 1920s. (p. 80)

Collection of Mrs Martha Hare

Gouache on paper, $8\frac{5}{8} \times 6\frac{3}{4}$ in. (21.9 × 17.2 cm.). Stamped at lower right: Gwen John (estate stamp)

PROVENANCE: estate of the artist (E.J.156), until 1958; private collection, 1958; Christie's, London, 28 February 1975, lot 71; Davis & Long, 1975–7

LITERATURE: Langdale, no. 321

See note to Cat. 78 (*Seated Nun and Standing Woman in Church*).

115. *A Girl with Long Hair Kneeling in Church, Seen from Behind.* Probably 1920s. (p. 66)

Cardiff, National Museum of Wales

Gouache and pencil on paper, $6\frac{1}{2} \times 5$ in. (16.5 × 12.7 cm.)

PROVENANCE: estate of the artist, until 1976

See note to Cat. 78 (*Seated Nun and Standing Woman in Church*).

116. *A Nun and Two Girls in Church.* Probably 1920s. (p. 62*)

Private collection

Gouache on paper, $6\frac{3}{8} \times 4\frac{7}{8}$ in. (16.2 × 12.4 cm.). Stamped at lower left: Gwen John (estate stamp)

PROVENANCE: estate of the artist (E.J.412), until 1966; via Faerber and Maison, to present owner

LITERATURE: Langdale, no. 315

See note to Cat. 78 (*Seated Nun and Standing Woman in Church*).

117. *A Girl Wearing a Hat and Coat with a Fur Collar, Seated in Church*. Probably 1920s. (p. 67)

Cardiff, National Museum of Wales

Gouache on paper, $6\frac{1}{2} \times 6\frac{1}{4}$ in. (16.5 × 15.9 cm.)

PROVENANCE: estate of the artist, until 1976

See note to Cat. 78 (*Seated Nun and Standing Woman in Church*).

118. *Petit Profil*. Probably 1920s. (p. 63*)

Collection of Mimi and Sanford Feld

Gouache on paper, $6\frac{5}{8} \times 6\frac{1}{8}$ in. (16.8 × 15.6 cm.). Stamped at lower left: Gwen John (estate stamp)

PROVENANCE: estate of the artist (E.J.521), until 1970; via Faerber and Maison, to Davis, 1970; private collection, until 1978

See note to Cat. 78 (*Seated Nun and Standing Woman in Church*).

119. *Little Girl in Check Coat with Woman in Black*. Probably 1920s. (p. 62*)

Private collection

Gouache and watercolour on paper, $4\frac{3}{4} \times 4$ in. (12.1 × 10.2 cm.)

PROVENANCE: estate of the artist (E.J.902), until 1982; via d'Offay, to present owner

See note to Cat. 78 (*Seated Nun and Standing Woman in Church*).

120. *Les Chapeaux à Brides*. Probably late 1920s. (p. 80)

Collection of Mimi and Sanford Feld

Gouache on paper, $4 \times 4\frac{3}{8}$ in. (10.3 × 11.1 cm.). Stamped at lower left: Gwen John (estate stamp)

PROVENANCE: estate of the artist (E.J.723); via d'Offay, to Davis & Langdale, as of 1981

LITERATURE: Langdale, no. 334

See note to Cat. 78 (*Seated Nun and Standing Woman in Church*).

121. *The Victorian Sisters*. Probably *c*.1928–33. (p. 81)

Private collection

Gouache, watercolour, and pencil on paper, $6\frac{3}{8} \times 4\frac{7}{8}$ in. (16.2 × 12.4 cm.). Stamped at lower left: estate stamp

PROVENANCE: estate of the artist (E.J.815), until 1977; via d'Offay, to present owner

*The Victorian Sisters* is based upon a 1926 prayer card of an 1876 photograph of Ste. Thérèse de Lisieux (1873–97) at the age of three and a half, with a child who is presumably her older sister. Sheets of sketches of the composition bear dates from 1928–33.

122. *Seated Girl Holding a Child*. Probably *c*.1929–31. (p. 71)

Private collection

Gouache on paper, $4\frac{1}{8} \times 5\frac{3}{8}$ in. (10.5 × 13.6 cm.). Stamped at lower right: Gwen John (estate stamp)

PROVENANCE: estate of the artist (E.J.967), until 1982; via d'Offay, to present owner

LITERATURE: Langdale, no. 346

Sheets of studies of this composition are dated 1929, 1930 and 1931.

123. *Woman in a Railway Carriage*. Probably late 1920s to early 1930s. (p. 80)

Private collection

Gouache and pencil on paper, $8\frac{3}{4} \times 6\frac{7}{8}$ in. (22.2 × 17.5 cm.)

PROVENANCE: estate of the artist (E.J.618), until 1982; via d'Offay, to present owner

124. *Flowers in Jug*. Probably *c*.1930. (p. 79)

Private collection

Gouache on paper, $6\frac{3}{8} \times 4\frac{3}{4}$ in. (16.2 × 12 cm.). Stamped at lower left: Gwen John (estate stamp)

PROVENANCE: estate of the artist (E.J.426), until 1969; via Faerber and Maison, to Davis; private collection, until 1975; Davis & Long, until 1977

A sheet of studies for this composition is dated 1930.

125. *Trees*. *c*.1928. (p. 78)

Cardiff, National Museum of Wales

Gouache, $9\frac{3}{4} \times 8\frac{3}{4}$ in. (24.8 × 22.2 cm.)

PROVENANCE: estate of the artist, until 1976

126. *Head of Seated Girl in Church, Seen from Behind*. Set of six. 1920s. (p. 81)

Cardiff, National Museum of Wales

**a**. Black chalk on buff paper, $6\frac{1}{2} \times 5$ in. (16.5 × 12.7 cm.) **b**. Black chalk on buff paper, $6\frac{1}{2} \times 5$ in. (16.5 × 12.7 cm.) **c**. Watercolour, $5\frac{3}{8} \times 4\frac{1}{4}$ in. (13.7 × 10.8 cm.) **d**. Watercolour, $5\frac{1}{2} \times 4\frac{1}{4}$ in. (14 × 10.8 cm.) **e**. Watercolour and black chalk, $6\frac{1}{2} \times 5$ in. (16.5 × 12.7 cm.) **f**. Watercolour and black chalk, $6\frac{1}{2} \times 5$ in. (16.5 × 12.7 cm.)

PROVENANCE: estate of the artist, until 1976

## Selected Exhibitions

Exhibitions took place in London, unless stated otherwise. Abbreviations used in the catalogue appear in bold type.

1903 **Carfax 1903** Carfax & Co. Ltd., *Paintings, Pastels and Etchings by Augustus E. John. Paintings by Gwendolen M. John.*

1925 **NEAC, London, 1925** New English Art Club, *The New English Art Club Special Retrospective Exhibition 1886–1924.*

1925 **NEAC, Manchester, 1925** City of Manchester Art Gallery, *The New English Art Club Special Retrospective Exhibition 1886–1924.*

1926 **Art Center, 1926** The Art Center, New York, *Memorial Exhibition of Representative Works Selected from the John Quinn Collection: Paintings, Water Colors, and Sculpture Selected from the John Quinn Collection.*

1926 **Chenil, 1926** The New Chenil Galleries, *Paintings and Drawings by Gwen John.*

1946 Matthiesen Ltd., *Gwen John Memorial Exhibition.* Catalogue introduction by Augustus John.

1946 Arts Council of Great Britain, *Gwen John.*

1952 Tate Gallery, *Ethel Walker, Frances Hodgkins, Gwen John. A Memorial Exhibition.* Catalogue introduction by John Rothenstein.

1958 Matthiesen Gallery, *Gwen John.*

1961 Matthiesen Gallery, *Gwen John.* Catalogue introduction by Myfanwy Piper.

1961 Faerber & Maison Ltd., *Gwen John.* Catalogue introduction by Mary Taubman.

1968 Arts Council of Great Britain, *Gwen John. A Retrospective Exhibition.* Catalogue introduction by Mary Taubman. Shown in London, Sheffield and Cardiff.

1970 Faerber & Maison Ltd., *Gwen John.* Catalogue introduction by Stefanie Maison.

1975 Davis & Long Company, Inc., New York, *Gwen John. A Retrospective Exhibition.* Catalogue introduction by Cecily Langdale.

1976 Anthony d'Offay Ltd., *Gwen John.* Catalogue introduction by Mary Taubman.

1976 National Museum of Wales, Cardiff, *Gwen John Centenary Exhibition.* Catalogue introduction by A. D. Fraser Jenkins.

1982 Stanford University Museum of Art, Stanford, California, *Gwen John: Paintings and Drawings from the Collection of John Quinn and Others.* Catalogue essays: 'Gwen John and her Patron John Quinn' by Betsy G. Fryberger; 'Gwen John's Paintings' by Cecily Langdale.

1982 Anthony d'Offay Ltd., *Gwen John.* Catalogue essay 'Gwen John: Artist in Exile' by Michael Holroyd.

## Galleries and Sales Abbreviated in the Catalogue

| | |
|---|---|
| **American Art Galleries, 1927** | American Art Galleries, New York, sale, 9–12 February 1927, *Paintings and Sculpture: The Renowned Collection of Modern and Ultra-Modern Art Formed by the late John Quinn.* |
| **Davis** | Davis Galleries, New York. |
| **Davis & Langdale** | Davis & Langdale Company, Inc., New York. |
| **Davis & Long** | Davis & Long Company, Inc., New York. |
| **d'Offay** | Anthony d'Offay Ltd., London. |
| **Faerber & Maison** | Faerber and Maison Ltd., London. |
| **Matthiesen** | Matthiesen Ltd., London. |
| NEAC | New English Art Club, London. |

## Selected Bibliography


BARR, ALFRED H., Jr., 'Modern Art in London Museums', *The Arts*, vol. XIV, no. 4, October 1928, pp. 190, 194.

CHAMOT, M., 'An Undiscovered Artist. Gwen John', *Country Life*, 19 June 1926, pp. 884–5.

CHITTY, SUSAN, *Gwen John*, 1981.

HOLROYD, MICHAEL, *Augustus John*, vol. I 1974, vol. II 1975.

JOHN, AUGUSTUS, 'Gwendolen John', *Burlington Magazine*, 1942, 81, pp. 236–7.

JOHN, AUGUSTUS, *Chiaroscuro. Fragments of Autobiography: First Series*, 1952.

*The John Quinn Collection of Paintings, Water Colors, Drawings and Sculpture*, 1926.

LANGDALE, CECILY, *Gwen John: A Catalogue Raisonné of the Paintings and a Selection of the Drawings*, to be published by Yale University Press, 1986.

LEWIS, WYNDHAM, 'The Art of Gwen John', the *Listener*, 10 October 1946, p. 484.

PALMER, J. WOOD, 'Gwen John', *Studio*, vol. 134, no. 656, November 1947, pp. 138–9.

REID, B. L., *The Man from New York: John Quinn and his Friends*, 1968.

ROTHENSTEIN, JOHN, 'Gwen John', *Modern English Painters*, 1952, vol. I.

ROTHENSTEIN, WILLIAM, *Men and Memories*, vol. I 1931, vol. II 1932.

ROWAN, ERIC, 'The Fire and the Fountain', the *Listener*, 20 March 1975.

TWITCHIN, ANNELA, *Gwen John, her Art and her Religion*, MA Report, Courtauld Institute of Art, May 1972.

## Lenders

E. Pace Barnes, 52, 103; Bedford, the Trustees of the Cecil Higgins Art Gallery, 94; Birmingham City Museum and Art Gallery, 26; Buffalo, Albright-Knox Art Gallery, 41, 74; Carter Burden, 47, 77, 80, 86, 109; Cambridge, Fitzwilliam Museum, 101; Cardiff, National Museum of Wales, 25, 38, 53, 64, 108, 110, 111, 115, 117, 125, 126; Terry Davis, 69, 91; the Duke of Devonshire, 99; Dublin, The Hugh Lane Municipal Gallery of Modern Art, 32; Estate of the artist, c/o Anthony d'Offay, 27, 50; Mimi and Sanford Feld, 118, 120; Mrs Martha Hare, 82, 112, 114; Helena D. Henderson, 9; Ben John, 36, 45, 104; Howard Kopet, 63, 76; Leeds City Art Galleries, 14; Mr and Mrs D. Little, 51; London, the Trustees of the British Museum, 58; National Portrait Gallery, 5; the Trustees of the Tate Gallery, 4, 7, 8, 12, 29, 59, 62; Victoria and Albert Museum, 61, 96; Manchester City Art Galleries, 6, 22, 43, 44; University of Manchester, Whitworth Art Gallery, 106; Melbourne, National Gallery of Victoria, 3, 18; Paul Mellon Collection, Upperville, Virginia, 30, 35, 39; New York, Metropolitan Museum of Art, 2, 28; The Museum of Modern Art, 13, 15, 48; Northampton, Smith College Museum of Art, 31; Paris, Musée Rodin, 67; Mrs R. Pilkington, 33; Private collections, 1, 11, 16, 17, 21, 23, 24, 34, 37, 40, 42, 46, 49, 54, 56, 57, 60, 65, 66, 71, 72, 73, 75, 78, 83, 84, 85, 87, 88, 89, 90, 92, 93, 95, 97, 98, 100, 102, 105, 107, 113, 116, 119, 121, 122, 123, 124; Sheffield City Art Galleries, 10, 55; Southampton Art Gallery, 20; Stanford University Museum of Art, 79, 81; Swindon, Borough of Thamesdown Museums and Art Gallery, 70; Yale University Art Gallery, 19, 68.

## Photographic Acknowledgements

We would like to thank the above named, and also the following, for supplying photographs and for allowing us to reproduce them: Ashmolean Museum, Oxford; Birmingham City Museum and Art Gallery; Bradford City Art Gallery; Geoffrey Clements; A. C. Cooper Ltd.; Prudence Cuming Associates Ltd.; Anthony d'Offay Gallery; Fitzwilliam Museum, Cambridge; Freer Art Gallery, Washington; Helga Photo Studios Inc.; Hilly Hoar; Michael Holroyd; Ben John; Cecily Langdale; Leeds City Art Gallery; Ludwig L. Roselius Sammlung, Bremen; Manchester City Art Galleries; Musée Rodin, Paris; National Museum of Wales, Cardiff; Studio Nine Inc.; Ellen Page Wilson.

# Index